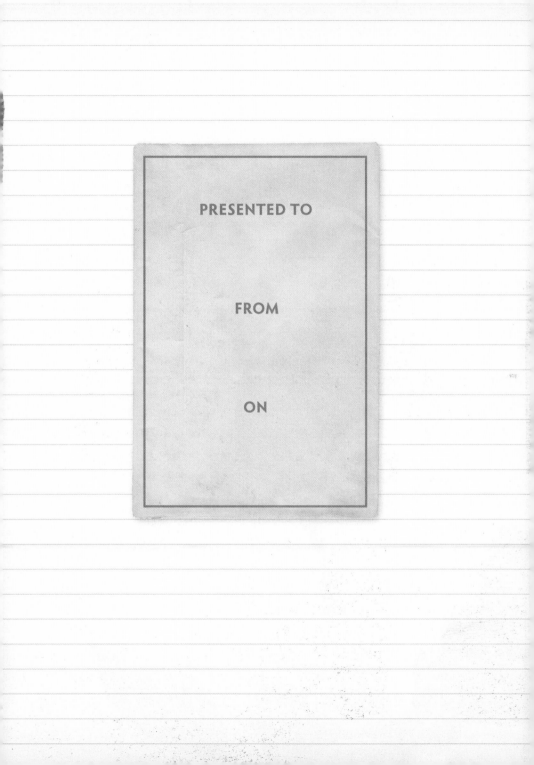

PRESENTED TO

FROM

ON

52 Life-Changing Questions

CALLED
to inspire

Marsha DuCille

Tyndale House Publishers, Inc.
Carol Stream, Illinois

LIVING EXPRESSIONS COLLECTION

Living Expressions invites you to explore God's Word and express your creativity in ways that are refreshing to the spirit and restorative to the soul.

Visit Tyndale online at www.tyndale.com.

Visit *CALLED* magazine at www.calledmagazine.com.

TYNDALE, Tyndale's quill logo, *Living Expressions*, and the Living Expressions logo are registered trademarks of Tyndale House Publishers, Inc.

CALLED to Inspire: 52 Life-Changing Questions

Designed by Libby Dykstra

For information about special discounts for bulk purchases, please contact Tyndale House Publishers at csresponse@tyndale.com, or call 1-800-323-9400.

ISBN 978-1-4964-3598-9

Printed in China

25 24 23 22 21 20 19
7   6   5   4   3   2   1

CONTENTS

Introduction 1

1. What Does It Mean? 2
2. Do You Accept the Definition? 6
3. Are You Bound? 10
4. How Many Regrets? 14
5. Will You Listen? 18
6. Is Lazarus Dead? 22
7. What Does God Think of Women? 26
8. Is He Too Busy? 30
9. Have You Made Rest a Priority? 34
10. Can God Invest in You? 38
11. What Do You Have? 42
12. Are You Skilled? 46
13. How Heavy Is the Load? 50
14. How Big Is Your Army? 56
15. Whose Armor Are You Wearing? 60
16. Is the Gate Guarded? 64
17. Is It a Bowl of Stew? 68
18. Have You Applied Discipline? 72
19. Is It a Distraction? 76
20. Do You Follow the Trend? 80
21. Who Has the Power? 84
22. Where Do You Go? 88
23. What Did You Say? 92
24. Is the Baby Protected? 96
25. What Has Passed Down? 100

26. What Do You Really Want? 104

27. Will You Seek Vengeance? 110

28. Does It Hurt? 114

29. Too Hard to Love? 118

30. Have You Asked? 122

31. Whose Voice Is That? 126

32. Did You Hear the Whisper? 130

33. How Do You Talk to Yourself? 134

34. Are You Martha? 138

35. Do You Give Honor? 142

36. Where Is the Compassion? 146

37. Are You Sincere? 150

38. Is Forgiveness Too Free? 154

39. Are Strings Attached? 158

40. Is It Your Business? 164

41. Why Compare? 168

42. What Is the Season? 172

43. Will You Take This Blessing? 176

44. Are You Intentionally Intimate? 180

45. Have You Embraced the Process? 184

46. Is He Absent? 188

47. Will You Pick Yourself Up? 192

48. Should You Try Another Way? 196

49. What Is Joy? 200

50. Have You Given Thanks? 204

51. Will You Win or Lose? 208

52. What Are You Waiting For? 212

Notes 216

About the Author 218

INTRODUCTION

IN 2007, WHEN I LAUNCHED *CALLED* MAGAZINE, my life was headed in a different direction. My plan was to practice law and shape public policy. *Me? Start a Christian magazine? God had to be out of his mind!* But the Lord is an out-of-the-box God with out-of-the-box ideas, and he's constantly stretching us to new heights. So when the Lord decided to call my name, I boldly dared to answer.

God has called *you* to do something special, and the world is waiting. If you feel weak, fearful, or unprepared, *CALLED to Inspire* will guide you along the way. Each chapter presents a life-changing question that every woman should answer. The Bible-based devotionals delve into real-life issues—because your journey demands real-life answers. There's also a prayer, declaration, and journal prompt included with every chapter.

CALLED to Inspire was written especially for you. *Don't you hear the Lord calling your name?* You can cling to this companion week after week—and dare to render your answer.

~Marsha DuCille

1. What Does It Mean?

THE BIBLE IS FASCINATING FOR MANY REASONS, but the diversity of its characters makes it remarkable. Kings and queens, believers and doubters. Virgins and prostitutes, saints and liars. Through the Word of God, we come face-to-face with the triumphs of imperfect people who dared to answer their call.

Being "called" doesn't mean that we're perfect or even qualified. It simply means that God has a purpose for our lives. It also means that he has a plan for *everything* in our lives. It can be hard to fathom God's purpose for our hardships, but the Bible teaches that God always has a greater plan: "We can rejoice, too, when we run into problems and trials, for we know that they help us develop endurance. And endurance develops strength of character, and character strengthens our confident hope of salvation" (Romans 5:3-4).

I marvel when I think of Harriet Tubman's calling. Born a slave, she escaped to freedom and became the most renowned "conductor" of the Underground Railroad. The appalling conditions of slavery offered only two reasonable options: *freedom or death.* After Harriet escaped, she returned to the South a myriad of times and escorted hundreds of slaves to freedom. Abolitionist William Lloyd Garrison called Harriet the "Moses" of her people.

Like Harriet Tubman, you are called to do something special for God, so dare to do it! It might be hard to imagine, but even your struggles are paving the way to your purpose. Therefore, don't be bound by your past or enchained by your limitations. Let the Lord set you free. For in due time, your freedom will free many others.

PRAYER

Dear Lord,

Set me free from everything that keeps me from fulfilling my purpose.

In Jesus' name, amen.

STRENGTH IN THE WORD

The old life is gone; a new life has begun!

2 CORINTHIANS 5:17

TODAY I DECLARE

God has a calling on my life, and I will answer it.

▼ JOURNAL ENTRY

What do you sense God calling you to do?
Write down your dreams and passions.

Journal away!

* KEEPSAKE
"Let the Lord set you free."

2. Do You Accept the Definition?

IF I WERE TO ASK YOU TO LIST YOUR GIFTS, you would likely name attributes that someone brought to your attention. Maybe a teacher praised you for being a math whiz or a skilled writer. Perhaps a relative called you an excellent cook or a beautiful singer. The positive words spoken over our lives influence what we call ourselves. In fact, the opposite is also true. Some adults are still trapped by the characterizations that they were given as children. Even as grown-ups, the deprecating voice of a parent or teacher continues to hold them back.

In 1 Chronicles 4:9-10, Jabez refused to accept his mother's negative definition of who he was. Because of her insufferable labor pains, she named him Jabez, meaning "He will cause pain." Jabez's name announced that he was a conveyer of grief, not a source of joy; he was an affliction, not a blessing. But Jabez prayed and asked God to redefine his name: "'Oh, that you would bless me and expand my territory! Please be with me in all that I do, and keep me from all trouble and pain!' And God granted him his request."

I don't know what you've been called in the past, but the only definition that matters is the one that God gives you—and the one that you give yourself. You have the power to define your name. If you've been called a failure, redefine yourself as a *winner*. If you've been called broke, redefine yourself as *prosperous*. If you've been called unloved, redefine yourself as *treasured*. Today, you can replace every negative definition.

⚱ PRAYER

Dear Lord,

Strip me of every negative definition that's been spoken over my life.

In Jesus' name, amen.

►◄ STRENGTH IN THE WORD

Thank you for making me so wonderfully complex! Your workmanship is marvelous.

PSALM 139:14

◄► TODAY I DECLARE

Other people won't define me.

▼ JOURNAL ENTRY

How do *you* define yourself?

Journal away!

* KEEPSAKE
"*You have the power to define your name.*"

3. Are You Bound?

AT ONE POINT OR ANOTHER, we've all been pinned "between a rock and a hard place." Yet few of us would be willing to amputate an arm in order to be set free. But that's what Aron Ralston did—with a dull pocketknife. While he was climbing over heavy boulders in his hiking path, one of them rolled and trapped his right hand. Five days after unsuccessfully trying to free himself, Aron cut off his right forearm to save his life. It's a true story that's documented in his memoir, *Between a Rock and a Hard Place*, and it's the subject of the Oscar-nominated film *127 Hours*.

Aron Ralston had to choose between the arm that he wanted and the life that he needed. Our spiritual choices face a similar crossroad. There will be things that we want to keep (like relationships and habits), but God will ask us to let them go. The freeing decision will be a matter of spiritual life or death. In Matthew 5:30, Jesus instructs, "If your hand—even your stronger hand—causes you to sin, cut it off and throw it away. It is better for you to lose one part of your body than for your whole body to be thrown into hell."

When we're bound, we're unable to break free from the sin that holds us back. But Matthew 5:30 commands that we find a way to cut those things off and throw them away—removing the possibility of changing our minds and being bound again.

At times, you'll have to sever relationships that you want to keep and cut off habits that help you cope. But Aron Ralston cut off his arm to save his natural life, and you must cut off whatever is necessary to save your spiritual life.

⚡ PRAYER

Dear Lord,

Show me the parts of
my life that must go.

In Jesus' name, amen.

►◄ STRENGTH
IN THE WORD

I will walk in freedom.

PSALM 119:45

◄► TODAY I DECLARE

No habit or relationship is
worth my spiritual freedom.

How do you define spiritual freedom?

Journal away!

* KEEPSAKE
"Break free from the sin."

4. How Many Regrets?

A SINGLE, MIDDLE-AGED PASTOR once told me that he fell in love with a woman during his twenties, but he didn't marry her. Although she brought him joy in a thrilling and unexpected way, he couldn't picture her as a pastor's wife.

She was rough around the edges; not exactly the Bible-teaching type. Moreover, he wondered, *What would other ministers think?* His wife would need to play a role, and she would be expected to look the part. Subsequently, the pastor's "true love" married someone else—and he regrets that misfortune every day of his life.

People pleasers have many regrets, because their lives aren't their own. Like parched wanderers in a desert, they roam in whatever direction satisfies their thirst. It can be a never-ending quest for approval. But those who drink the water that Jesus gives "will never be thirsty again" (John 4:14).

With the Lord's cup of affirmation, you can charge forward in any direction your destiny takes you. And you'll need it, because God has a track record for requesting unusual things. He instructed Hosea to marry a prostitute and told Noah to build a massive ark. *"A flood?"* people surely quipped—as Noah invested hefty resources into building a 450-foot boat over the course of decades. But "Noah did everything exactly as God had commanded him" (Genesis 6:22).

The apostle Paul wrote, "I'm not trying to win the approval of people, but of God" (Galatians 1:10). Therefore, drink the cup of affirmation that Jesus gives, and charge forward with your destiny. You'll have far fewer regrets as a God pleaser.

⚕ PRAYER

Dear Lord,

Deliver me from the fear
of what people think,
say, and do.

In Jesus' name, amen.

►◄ STRENGTH
IN THE WORD

Fearing people is a
dangerous trap.

PROVERBS 29:25

◄► TODAY I DECLARE

God's validation is
more than enough.

▼ JOURNAL ENTRY

If God asked you to build a massive ark in the middle
of a desert, would you dare to do it?

Journal away!

✳ KEEPSAKE
*"God has a track record for
requesting unusual things."*

5. Will You Listen?

THE BIBLICAL STORY OF BALAAM is fit for a Disney film. It has all the necessary characters: a talking donkey, a shady prophet, and an invisible angel. But between the kiddie enchantment and enthralling plot, there's something deeper.

Throughout the years, my most helpful customers have been the unpleasant ones. They never fail to point out what "sweeter" folks won't mention. Sure, their messages usually sting, but they also guide me in a better direction. In the Bible, God used a donkey to deliver a message to the prophet Balaam. And God will use anyone to deliver a message to you.

When Balaam was headed down a road (going somewhere that God didn't approve of), his donkey stopped because an angel was blocking the way. Unable to see this, Balaam beat the animal three times. "Then the LORD gave the donkey the ability to speak"—*which certainly got Balaam's attention!* Soon after, "the LORD opened Balaam's eyes, and he saw the angel of the LORD standing in the roadway. . . . 'Look,'" the angel said, "'I have come to block your way because you are stubbornly resisting me. Three times the donkey saw me and shied away; otherwise, I would certainly have killed you'" (Numbers 22:21-33).

In your animated film called *Life*, God will use a variety of characters to get your attention—like your critical mother or prying neighbor, because they have the guts to stop you in your tracks. So before you attack them, the way Balaam beat his donkey, ask the Lord to open your eyes. There's possibly something in the road that you can't see.

⏳ PRAYER

Dear Lord,
Use whomever you wish
to get my attention.
In Jesus' name, amen.

►◄ STRENGTH
IN THE WORD

Fools think their own
way is right, but the
wise listen to others.

PROVERBS 12:15

◄► TODAY I DECLARE

I will be more receptive
and less defensive.

▼ JOURNAL ENTRY

How do you define "constructive" and "destructive" criticism?

Journal away!

* KEEPSAKE

"God will use anyone to deliver a message."

6. Is Lazarus Dead?

ONE OF *CALLED* MAGAZINE'S READERS ONCE WROTE, "My dream function has been broken." Age can make us feel this way. As the years progress, people tend to think that they've wasted too much time. But you're not too old, and it's not too late to accomplish your dream.

Anna Mary Robertson Moses, better known as "Grandma Moses," began her painting career in her mid-seventies. In her golden years, she painted thousands of creations—including twenty-five after the age of one hundred. Some of the finest museums in the world have displayed Grandma Moses' paintings, and various reproductions have been placed on china, fabrics, tiles, and greeting cards. In 1946, 16 million of her Christmas cards were sold, and one of her paintings was purchased for $1.2 million in 2006. *Do you still think you're too old?*

Through your faith, God can resurrect your dream, just as through the words of Jesus, God resurrected Lazarus: "When Jesus arrived at Bethany, he was told that Lazarus had already been in his grave for four days." However, Jesus said to Martha, "Your brother will rise again."

"Lord, he has been dead for four days. The smell will be terrible," Martha protested. But Jesus replied, "Didn't I tell you that you would see God's glory if you believe?" With great authority, Jesus then shouted, "Lazarus, come out!" And the dead man rose (John 11:17-44).

Your dream may have died years ago, but it can live again. So tell your Lazarus to rise! You're not too old, and it's not too late to fully live your life.

✷ PRAYER

Dear Lord,
Resurrect the dormant
passions of my heart.
In Jesus' name, amen.

►◄ STRENGTH
IN THE WORD

Take delight in the LORD,
and he will give you
your heart's desires.

PSALM 37:4

◄► TODAY I DECLARE

My dream will live again.

▼ JOURNAL ENTRY

What is your dream?

Journal away!

* KEEPSAKE

"Tell your Lazarus to rise!"

7. What Does God Think of Women?

MANY RELIGIOUS GROUPS HAVE LONG QUESTIONED the value of women. In the Middle East, where Jesus lived, Jewish rabbis began every synagogue meeting with this prayer of thanksgiving: "Blessed art Thou, O Lord our God, King of the Universe, who *hast not* made me a woman." To this day, women are sometimes treated like second-class citizens at their places of worship. But God responded to the petition of Zelophehad's daughters and answered this question: *Does he value women?*

Zelophehad died during the forty years that the Israelites were wandering through the wilderness. With five daughters and no sons, his children couldn't inherit his land. The laws and customs of the time denied women inheritance rights. In fact, women themselves were considered to *be* property.

However, the five sisters—Mahlah, Noah, Hoglah, Milcah, and Tirzah—boldly "stood before Moses, Eleazar the priest, the tribal leaders, and the entire community," and they petitioned for their rights. "Why should the name of our father disappear from his clan just because he had no sons?" the sisters asked. "Give us property along with the rest of our relatives." So Moses took their case before God, and the Lord replied, "The claim of the daughters of Zelophehad is legitimate. You must give them a grant of land along with their father's relatives. Assign them the property that would have been given to their father" (Numbers 27:1-7). *Hello, women's rights!*

Unfairness of any kind can make the best of us feel inferior; but God values women. We can boldly go before the throne of God and collect our inheritance. "Blessed art Thou, O Lord our God, King of the Universe, who *hast* made me a woman."

⅄ PRAYER

Dear Lord,

Help me to see my value,
no matter how I am treated.

In Jesus' name, amen.

►◄ STRENGTH IN THE WORD

There is no longer Jew or
Gentile, slave or free, male
and female. For you are
all one in Christ.

GALATIANS 3:28

◄► TODAY I DECLARE

I am an important
and valued heir in
God's Kingdom.

Read the encounter between Jesus and the Samaritan woman
(John 4:1-30). What does it reveal about his perception of women?

Journal away!

* KEEPSAKE

*"We can boldly collect
our inheritance."*

8. Is He Too Busy?

PSALM 37:23 IS ONE OF MY FAVORITE SCRIPTURES: "The LORD directs the steps of the godly. He delights in every detail of their lives." The phrase "every detail" always brings me comfort because it's an invitation to include God in every crevice. It also teaches us that God doesn't operate like people. Generally, the bigger a person becomes—in stature and power—the less they're willing to get involved in "minor" things. This human tendency can make us believe that *God* is too busy for the lighter matters in our lives; however, that isn't true.

We've been correctly taught that nothing is too big for God, but that shouldn't lead us to believe that he only handles big things. Yes, there are starving children in this world (which is a global dilemma), but that doesn't lessen the loneliness that you might feel, nor does it diminish the "small" desires of your heart. The Bible states that God "delights in every detail." That literally means he takes *great pleasure* in all things that concern you. (*Have you ever prayed for a parking spot? Yep, God took pleasure in being a part of that process.*) In fact, Jesus' first miracle was turning water into wine at a wedding in the village of Cana in Galilee. No one was dying, no children were starving, and no one was lame. Yet, Jesus delivered a miracle—for the sole enjoyment of the guests (John 2:1-11).

Don't ever believe that God is too busy for anything concerning you, big or small. Psalm 37:23 invites you to welcome him into every single, itty-bitty area of your life. He delights in it all.

⚓ PRAYER

Dear Lord,

Walk with me, side by side,
every second of the day.
I welcome you in.

In Jesus' name, amen.

►◄ STRENGTH IN THE WORD

The LORD would speak to
Moses face to face, as one
speaks to a friend.

EXODUS 33:11

◄► TODAY I DECLARE

God is always interested
and always available.

▼ JOURNAL ENTRY

What do you love most about your friendship with God?

Journal away!

＊ KEEPSAKE
"Include God in every crevice."

9. Have You Made Rest a Priority?

A LOT OF WOMEN SUFFER from the same chronic condition: exhaustion. They believe they're doing *nothing* when they're resting—but they're wrong.

Rest is one of the hardest things to define, and an even harder thing to do. The average person thinks rest is sleep; however, someone can sleep an entire day, yet still feel exhausted. But rest—*the detoxing and refueling of our spirits*—is the result of unplugging from the world and plugging into God. It's so spiritually critical that God took the time to make it sacred. Genesis 2:2-3 states, "On the seventh day God had finished his work of creation, so he rested. . . . God blessed the seventh day and declared it holy, because it was the day when he rested."

How could a God with infinite strength need rest? Well, he didn't. God rested for us. By setting the example, the Lord was essentially saying, *Rest isn't for the weak. It's for the strong.* It takes strength to disconnect from a world that bellows, *People who rest miss out.*

But the opposite is true. In 1946, Chick-fil-A founder Truett Cathy decided to close his restaurant on Sundays to give employees a day of spiritual rest. Industry insiders thought it was madness. Surely a restaurant couldn't thrive if it remained closed on one of the busiest days of the week. But Chick-fil-A did! A 2016 report indicated that, since 2010, Chick-fil-A had led the fast-food industry in average sales per restaurant.

When we make rest a priority—by shutting off the world and plugging into God—the Lord detoxes and refuels our spirits. He also helps us do more with less time.

PRAYER

Dear Lord,
Replenish my soul. As
a deer pants for water,
my soul pants for you.
In Jesus' name, amen.

STRENGTH
IN THE WORD

The Sabbath was made to
meet the needs of people.

MARK 2:27

TODAY I DECLARE

Rest is a necessity,
not an option.

▼ JOURNAL ENTRY

Take a leisurely walk with God and soak in the beauty of creation.
Describe what the experience does for your soul.

Journal away!

* KEEPSAKE
"God rested for us."

10. Can God Invest in You?

THIS MIGHT SOUND SACRILEGIOUS, but God is a shrewd investor. He sows wherever he will get a return. That's why certain people always have more. They take whatever God gives them and multiply it.

In Matthew 25:14-30, Jesus compares the Kingdom of Heaven to the Parable of the Three Servants: A man went on a trip and left his three servants in charge of his money. Each one was given an amount based on their *ability*—that is, their ability to produce. Like God, the master didn't use a system based on *equivalence*; nor did he use a system based on *potential*. Instead, the master distributed his property based on *proven productivity*. The two servants who received the most put their allotment to work and doubled it. But the servant who received the least "dug a hole in the ground and hid the master's money." When the master returned, he took what the wasteful servant had and gave it to the one who produced the most. The master said, "To those who use well what they are given, even more will be given, and they will have an abundance. But from those who do nothing, even what little they have will be taken away."

At the age of nineteen months, Helen Keller was struck with an unknown illness that left her deaf and blind. Yet despite these tremendous obstacles, she accomplished a great deal with what she had. Helen became a prolific author, world-renowned lecturer, and social reformer. And those are only a few of her accomplishments. She took what God gave her and multiplied it!

Now I ask: Can God invest *in you*?

☀ PRAYER

Dear Lord,

Expand my ingenuity and show me how to multiply all that you've invested in me.

In Jesus' name, amen.

►◄ STRENGTH IN THE WORD

He prunes the branches that do bear fruit so they will produce even more.

JOHN 15:1-2

◄► TODAY I DECLARE

Whatever God gives me, I will multiply.

▼ JOURNAL ENTRY

How can you maximize what you've been given?
Brainstorm ways to give the Lord a more abundant return.

Journal away!

* KEEPSAKE
"God is a shrewd investor."

11. What Do You Have?

GROWING UP, MY BROTHER AND I affectionately called our stepmother "MacGyver." If you're familiar with the 1980s TV series, you know what that means. MacGyver had a gift for solving complex problems with ordinary items. He defied impossibilities. Our stepmom, Suzanne, could turn a sparsely stocked, end-of-the-week pantry into a gourmet meal. The last bit of flour would be spun into sweet, fluffy *Guyanese bakes*; and two potatoes could become a heavenly curry dish. Suzanne always found a way to create something.

God specializes in turning whatever we have into whatever we need. He's the ultimate resourceful genius. The Lord can stretch your sparsely stocked bank account and create a solution out of anything. That's what he did for one poor widow.

In 2 Kings 4, a widow went to the prophet Elisha and cried, "'My husband who served you is dead. . . . But now a creditor has come, threatening to take my two sons as slaves.'

"'What can I do to help you?' Elisha asked. 'Tell me, what do you have in the house?'

"'Nothing at all, except a flask of olive oil,' she replied."

Elisha then instructed the widow to borrow empty jars, shut the door, and pour the oil into the containers. "So she did as she was told. . . . Soon every container was full to the brim!"

The widow initially told Elisha she had "nothing at all, except a flask of olive oil"—but the oil was all that she needed. The widow sold the oil and paid off her debts (2 Kings 4:1-7). Your circumstances may also seem bleak, but God has given you a solution. Like the widow, first you must shut the door to impossibilities and use whatever you have.

⚡ PRAYER

Dear Lord,

Open my eyes to the possibilities and show me what I can use.

In Jesus' name, amen.

►◄ STRENGTH IN THE WORD

I know that you can do anything, and no one can stop you.

JOB 42:2

◄► TODAY I DECLARE

I am a resourceful problem-solver.

▼ JOURNAL ENTRY

How can you MacGyver this week's budget and spend less?

(Yes, MacGyver is an actual verb.)

Journal away!

✳ KEEPSAKE

"God has given you a solution."

12. Are You Skilled?

WOULD YOU ASK A LOUSY CHEF to cater your wedding, or hire a clumsy dentist to perform your root canal? *Probably not!* You would likely find someone who is skilled at doing their job.

Believe it or not, excellence is a reoccurring theme in the Bible. It's presented as a gateway to opportunity. Proverbs 22:29 states, "Do you see any truly competent workers? They will serve kings rather than working for ordinary people." David is a good example! He was introduced to King Saul simply because he was a skilled musician (1 Samuel 16:14-21).

God has called us to be skilled at our crafts because excellence gives us a stronger platform. It not only empowers us to share the gospel; it also compels people to listen. Ask yourself, *Why do folks care what successful people think?* They care because they want what successful people have. It's that simple! As Christians, we must redefine the meaning of success. It's not mere "accomplishment" or "the acquisition of things." It's a powerful gateway to ministerial opportunity. Success entices people to ask, *"How do you have what you have?"* And subsequently, we can boldly answer, *"Because of Jesus! He is my Savior and source."*

Talent is given to us by God, but *skill* is something that we develop. When David was taking the Ark of the Covenant to Jerusalem, he selected his lead worshiper for one reason: "Kenaniah, the head Levite, was chosen as the choir leader because of his skill" (1 Chronicles 15:22). Therefore, become excellent at whatever you do. It will open doors to new ministerial opportunities.

PRAYER

Dear Lord,

When I'm tempted to cut corners, give me a hunger for excellence.

In Jesus' name, amen.

STRENGTH IN THE WORD

The LORD will make you the head and not the tail.

DEUTERONOMY 28:13

TODAY I DECLARE

I will not settle for mediocrity.

▼ JOURNAL ENTRY

Take an inventory of your skills and choose one
that you can develop at a higher level.

Journal away!

13. How Heavy Is the Load?

WHEN PEOPLE THINK OF BIRDS, *flying* typically comes to mind. But over time, some birds, such as ostriches, emus, kiwis, and penguins, lost their ability to fly. They simply got too heavy, according to a New Zealand study. Although they still have wings, they can no longer take flight.

The weight of our worries produces a similar effect. It prevents us from soaring by loading down our dreams: *What if I fail? What if I'm inadequate? What if I don't have the money?* But God seldom shows us the entire plan. He seems to take pleasure in stretching our faith. For example, Noah was instructed to build an ark when there was no rain in sight, and Abraham was asked to leave his cozy life in exchange for an uncertain inheritance. *Did they have their share of worries?* Sure! What reasonable person wouldn't? But Noah and Abraham knew that it's "impossible to please God without faith" (Hebrews 11:6).

Faith (your steadfast trust in God, despite what you can't see) lightens your load. It gives you the courage to release your worries and soar with your dreams. Sometimes, the Lord will ask you to follow him without showing you the map—or he might summon you to build a dream without revealing the source of your supply. In those moments, release the weight of your worries to God and choose to fly. "Look at the birds," Jesus encourages in his Sermon on the Mount. "They don't plant or harvest or store food in barns, for your heavenly Father feeds them. And aren't you far more valuable to him than they are?" (Matthew 6:26).

PRAYER

Dear Lord,
Take the load that weighs
me down, and let my
dreams take flight.
In Jesus' name, amen.

STRENGTH
IN THE WORD

Don't worry about anything;
instead, pray about everything.

PHILIPPIANS 4:6

TODAY I DECLARE

I release every worry to God.
He will make a way.

What are you worried about? Use this space to let it go.
Dare to soar to greater heights.

Journal away!

＊ KEEPSAKE
*"Release the weight of
your worries."*

BLESSED IS THE PERSON

WHO IS TOO BUSY

TO WORRY IN THE DAYTIME

AND TOO SLEEPY

TO WORRY AT NIGHT.

ATTRIBUTED TO LEO AIKMAN

14. How Big Is Your Army?

G OD HAS A HABIT OF CHOOSING the most unlikely people, from the most unexpected backgrounds, and with the least amount of resources. He favors this approach because, in the end, he gets all the glory. In Isaiah 43:7, the Lord says, "Bring all who claim me as their God, for I have made them for my glory."

The biblical account of Gideon is a great example. The Lord called him to free the Israelites from the vicious rule of the Midianites, but Gideon didn't feel equipped for the task: "'But Lord,' Gideon replied, 'how can I rescue Israel? My clan is the weakest in the whole tribe of Manasseh, and I am the least in my entire family!'" (Judges 6:15). While Gideon was looking at his limitations, God saw an opportunity to display his divine power. "The LORD said to Gideon, 'You have too many warriors with you. If I let all of you fight the Midianites, the Israelites will boast to me that they saved themselves by their own strength'" (Judges 7:2). So God reduced Gideon's army from thirty-two thousand to three hundred men! With only three hundred warriors and a good dose of faith, Gideon led the Israelites to victory.

God often applies this "army reducing" strategy to our lives. He strips away the things that steal his glory. *Just think about it:* If God gave you all the support and all the resources that you thought you needed, why would you lean on him—and how would he get all the glory? Therefore, stay encouraged if your support and resources are small. God is preparing you for a glorifying victory.

PRAYER

Dear Lord,
Use my life to magnify
your greatness. I am a
vessel for your use.
In Jesus' name, amen.

STRENGTH IN THE WORD

You are worthy, O Lord our
God, to receive glory and
honor and power.

REVELATION 4:11

TODAY I DECLARE

God is not limited by
the size of my army.

▼ JOURNAL ENTRY

Does it feel like your "army of support" has been reduced? Name
at least two *good things* that can result from your smaller army.
Journal away!

* KEEPSAKE
*"He strips away the things
that steal his glory."*

15. Whose Armor Are You Wearing?

WE LIVE IN A COPYCAT SOCIETY: People commonly set their sights on being the next so-and-so. While there's nothing wrong with having ambition or being inspired, God is too creative to make duplicates. In fact, not even identical twins are *identical*. They have different fingerprints and distinct personalities. Far superior to the likes of da Vinci, Rembrandt, Picasso, and van Gogh, God's ingenuity never runs dry. *So, how could you succeed at being someone else?* God created you to be an original—not an imitation.

When David was preparing to fight Goliath, King Saul tried to dress David in his armor. The king assumed that the shepherd boy needed to "look" like a warrior in order to be successful in battle. The Bible states, "Saul gave David his own armor—a bronze helmet and a coat of mail. David put it on, strapped the sword over it, and took a step or two to see what it was like. . . . 'I can't go in these,' he protested to Saul. 'I'm not used to them.' So David took them off" (1 Samuel 17:38-39).

David wasn't afraid to be who God created him to be. Although many would have jumped at the opportunity to "look" like the king, David took off Saul's armor. He courageously chose to be authentic. With his simple garb, sling, and stones, David victoriously slew Goliath. Likewise, you should be who God called you to be. Walk *your* walk and talk *your* talk. Build your success on the foundation of authenticity.

⚡ PRAYER

Dear Lord,

Strip away every pretentious
layer and dress me in the
armor that you've given me.

In Jesus' name, amen.

▸◂ STRENGTH
IN THE WORD

We are God's masterpiece.

EPHESIANS 2:10

◂▸ TODAY I DECLARE

I am proud of who
God created me to be.

▼ JOURNAL ENTRY

Take a look in the mirror and observe the masterpiece God created.
List the characteristics and passions that make you "you."

Journal away!

✱ KEEPSAKE
"God created you to be an original."

16. Is the Gate Guarded?

GATEKEEPERS PLAYED AN IMPORTANT ROLE in biblical times. As watchmen who protected the gates of cities, palaces, and temples, they monitored who entered and exited—shielding their turf from invasion. They also maintained order. After God's people returned from exile in Babylon, 212 gatekeepers were commissioned to guard the Temple of the Lord. Their responsibilities also included watching over the Temple's articles, furnishings, and supplies.

As women, we're also gatekeepers. God uses us to "keep watch" over our families—looking, listening, and detecting what enters and leaves our homes. The gift of discernment gives us the power to see danger before it strikes, and we certainly have a propensity for sensing when "something isn't right."

In Judges 13, God used a woman to unlock the gate to his vision. The angel of the Lord appeared to Manoah's wife and revealed God's plan to rescue Israel. The angel told the woman that she would have a son, and her son would deliver Israel from the Philistines. She was the gatekeeper who opened the door to God's plan. When the woman informed her husband, he asked the Lord to send the angel again—this time to give more instructions to them both.

But when the angel returned, he appeared to *the woman*. Judges 13:9 states, "God answered Manoah's prayer, and the angel of God appeared once again to his wife as she was sitting in the field. But her husband, Manoah, was not with her."

As gatekeepers, we're called to usher in God's vision and protect our turf. We also detect danger with our spiritual eyes and fight attacks with our prayers. Therefore, guard your gate! Don't neglect your post.

PRAYER

Dear Lord,
Chase away the trouble that
knocks at my family's gate.
In Jesus' name, amen.

STRENGTH
IN THE WORD

Open up, ancient gates!
Open up, ancient doors, and
let the King of glory enter.

PSALM 24:9

TODAY I DECLARE

Through prayer, I will
be a faithful gatekeeper
for my family.

Make a list of the goodness that you want to let into your home.
How can you open the gate to those things?

Journal away!

* KEEPSAKE

"God uses us to 'keep watch' over our families."

17. Is It a Bowl of Stew?

IT'S EASY TO JUDGE ESAU. After all, the guy sold his birthright to his brother for a bowl of stew. But when we scratch beneath the surface, there's an important lesson to grasp.

"One day when Jacob was cooking some stew, Esau arrived home from the wilderness exhausted and hungry. Esau said to Jacob, 'I'm starved! Give me some of that red stew!' . . .

"'All right,' Jacob replied, 'but trade me your rights as the firstborn son.'" So, Esau agreed (Genesis 25:29-33).

Foolish. Ridiculous. Call it whatever you want. But anything that makes us settle for less is a bowl of stew. Esau's hunger represents the temporary discomforts that cause us to forfeit God's best for our lives. In his dim-witted moment, Esau was hungry—and in our dim-witted moments, we're sometimes lonely, afraid, ego driven, or angry. There are people who give up their families and careers for a fleeting fit of rage (bowl of stew)—and there are folks who auction their dreams for a more certain, but wrong, path in life (bowl of stew).

Warren Buffett once gave up billions to satisfy his ego. After taking offense when a former CEO of Berkshire Hathaway didn't honor their business agreement, Buffett decided to buy a controlling portion of the company—for the sole pleasure of firing the CEO. At the time, Berkshire Hathaway was a struggling textile mill that required a fortune to turn around. The vindictive decision (bowl of stew) cost Buffett roughly $200 billion.

Short-term discomforts can lead to costly decisions. Though the exchange may satisfy an immediate desire, the price is God's best for your life. Don't settle for less.

PRAYER

Dear Lord,
Give me the strength to
endure my short-term
discomforts.
In Jesus' name, amen.

STRENGTH IN THE WORD

God blesses those who
patiently endure testing
and temptation.

JAMES 1:12

TODAY I DECLARE

I will choose God's best.

What "bowl of stew" are you sometimes tempted to take?

Journal away!

✳ KEEPSAKE

"Don't settle for less."

18. Have You Applied Discipline?

I WISH I HAD A DOLLAR for every lady who wanted to be the Proverbs 31 woman. I'd have more money than I could spend. But who can blame us for wanting to be the quintessential, godly standard? The Proverbs 31 woman was phenomenal in virtually every way: a dutiful wife; a profitable business woman; an attentive mother; a compassionate do-gooder—and she even made her own bedspreads! Yet in the expanse of these majestic qualities, people often overlook her strongest trait: *The woman was disciplined.*

The Bible describes the Proverbs 31 woman as a "hard worker" who "gets up before dawn," and "her lamp burns late into the night" (verses 15-18). She wasn't endowed with superpowers, nor does the Bible mention any special blessing from God. The Proverbs 31 woman was extraordinary because she lived a disciplined life.

It must have taken tremendous self-control to bring her husband "good, not harm, all the days of her life" (verse 12). And with all the bedspreads and linen garments she was making, the woman had to be tired! But each morning, she rose early; and each evening, she worked late.

Proverbs 13:4 cautions, "Lazy people want much but get little, but those who work hard will prosper." The Proverbs 31 woman is a depiction of what we can accomplish—but we have to be willing to do what she had to do—in order to acquire the abundance that she had.

PRAYER

Dear Lord,

My heart is willing, but my motivation is weak. Give me a passion for discipline.

In Jesus' name, amen.

STRENGTH
IN THE WORD

No discipline is enjoyable while it is happening—it's painful! But afterward there will be a peaceful harvest.

HEBREWS 12:11

TODAY I DECLARE

I'm willing to do what I have to do.

▼ JOURNAL ENTRY

What do you admire most about the Proverbs 31 woman?

Journal away!

✱ KEEPSAKE

"She lived a disciplined life."

19. Is It a Distraction?

DISTRACTIONS ARE ARGUABLY the devil's most effective tool. A phone call here, a few e-mails there, and "little interruptions" everywhere—that's why few things get done. Take an estimate of how many times you're distracted during the average day, and then multiply it by twenty-five. That's how many minutes you're actually losing. It takes approximately twenty-five minutes to return to a task after being interrupted, says Gloria Mark, a researcher at the University of California, Irvine. A "twenty-second peek" online doesn't take only twenty seconds. It really consumes about twenty-five minutes and twenty seconds!

When Nehemiah had almost finished rebuilding the wall around Jerusalem, his enemies tried to sabotage him with distractions. But Nehemiah remained focused. He stated, "Sanballat and Geshem sent a message asking me to meet them. . . . So I replied by sending this message to them: 'I am engaged in a great work, so I can't come. Why should I stop working to come and meet with you?' Four times they sent the same message, and each time I gave the same reply." When those distractions didn't work, Nehemiah's enemies tried even harder to stop him from finishing the wall. However, he stood strong and stated, "I continued the work with even greater determination" (Nehemiah 6:1-9).

The devil will use distractions in an attempt to derail you. There's nothing "little" about them. They may come disguised as a *little break* or *little peek*—but they're actually *big threats* to your productivity. Nehemiah had to continue his work with "greater determination," and so will you.

PRAYER

Dear Lord,

Help me to focus like a
laser beam on the tasks
that are most important.

In Jesus' name, amen.

STRENGTH
IN THE WORD

Look straight ahead,
and fix your eyes on
what lies before you.

PROVERBS 4:25

TODAY I DECLARE

I will stick to my task
until it gets done.

▼ JOURNAL ENTRY

What are the "little distractions" that usually keep you from getting things done? How can you resist them with greater determination?

Journal away!

✳ KEEPSAKE

"The devil uses distractions to derail you."

20. Do You Follow the Trend?

TRENDS ARE EVERYWHERE, even in churches. It's gotten so bad that some Christians mistake trendy phrases for Scriptures: *"God won't give you more than you can handle."* No, that's not in the Bible. *"God helps those who help themselves."* Nope, that's not in there either.

As a business owner, I constantly have to choose between what's trendy and what's biblical. And it's hard—because trends sell. While preparing to launch a new day planner for women, I struggled with the title. My team polled our magazine's readers; we did extensive market research; and I even asked a random woman at the post office what she thought. The struggle was, indeed, real! Finally, we narrowed it down to two options. One of the titles was loved by almost every hard-core Christian surveyed. To them, the title *felt* spiritual and *sounded* right. To me, it *felt* profitable and *sounded* marketable.

But I kept twisting and turning with the trendy title—because it wasn't quite biblical. It required that I give *heaven* credit for *God's* work. But heaven was merely a place, and God was our actual source. I tried to tell myself that it wasn't that deep; however, anything that didn't line up with the Bible *was* deep.

As Christians living in a trend-driven world, we must measure everything against the Word of God. The biggest church won't necessarily be a biblical church; the popular way will often be the wrong way; and things that *sound* spiritual may not actually *be* spiritual. "A time is coming when people will no longer listen to sound and wholesome teaching. They will follow their own desires," warns 2 Timothy 4:3. But God is calling us to resist the trend and follow truth.

PRAYER

Dear Lord,

Give me the strength to never compromise your Word.

In Jesus' name, amen.

STRENGTH IN THE WORD

It is sin to know what you ought to do and then not do it.

JAMES 4:17

TODAY I DECLARE

I will follow truth.

▼ JOURNAL ENTRY

What unbiblical trends have you observed within yourself
and other believers?

Journal away!

✳ KEEPSAKE

*"Measure everything against
the Word of God."*

21. Who Has the Power?

MY CAREER HAS INTRODUCED ME to a lot of personalities. You'd be shocked to learn some of the things that I've heard. I must admit, I viewed Christianity through rose-colored glasses when I launched *CALLED* magazine. I was a twenty-seven-year-old graduate student filled with idealism. Running a faith-based company would be a piece of cake, *right*? Everyone would be patient and humble. Envoys would be kind and courteous. I had no clue what I was facing, but reality woke me up very quickly.

On one occasion, someone tried to strong-arm me to get what she wanted. She stated that her client was "very powerful" in an attempt to threaten me. I will never forget my response. I was trembling inside, but my words were unwavering: *"If your client is more powerful than God, I need to quit my job and reassess my life. The Bible says that God has all power."* In that moment, I was also speaking to myself. I needed to be reminded that God, and God alone, has all power. Anything that we have is given to us by him.

Throughout your life, you'll face a variety of bullies in many shapes and forms. Goliath was a giant who tormented the Israelites and stood nine feet tall. In 1 Samuel 17:8, he said, "I am the Philistine champion, but you are only the servants of Saul." When the Israelites heard this, they were terrified. As a believer, you are a servant of the Most High God, and "no weapon turned against you will succeed" (Isaiah 54:17). When you face your Goliath, don't be afraid. God has all power, and he will protect you.

⚱ PRAYER

Dear Lord,

You are my fire wall of
protection. When I'm
afraid, give me courage.
In Jesus' name, amen.

►◄ STRENGTH
IN THE WORD

Do not be afraid or
discouraged. For the
LORD your God is with
you wherever you go.

JOSHUA 1:9

◄► TODAY I DECLARE

With God by my side,
I will be strong and fearless.

▼ JOURNAL ENTRY

When someone tries to intimidate you, what is your gut reaction?

Journal away!

✱ KEEPSAKE

*"God, and God alone,
has all power."*

22. Where Do You Go?

WHEN A PRODUCT MALFUNCTIONS, we contact the manufacturer; and when a dish is burned, we send it back to the chef. Instinctively, we know to go straight to the source. God's promises work just like that. Every good and perfect gift comes from him (James 1:17). So when problems emerge, shouldn't we go straight to the Lord?

In 2 Kings 4:8-37, we learn about an extraordinary woman from the town of Shunem. Various translations call her *wealthy* or *prominent*. At her behest, she and her husband fed the prophet Elisha whenever he passed their way. They also built him a room and furnished it. Elisha declared a blessing over the Shunemite woman to show his gratitude, and he promised that she would give birth to a son. But though the boy was born within a year, he later died.

No reasonable person would fault the Shunemite woman if she had become troubled or angry. After all, Elisha's "blessing" appeared to be a curse. However, the Shunemite woman saw things differently. "She carried [her son] up and laid him on the bed of the man of God, then shut the door and left him there."

Next, she told her husband that she was going to see Elisha—she was going directly to the source. Her husband, perplexed, questioned what was going on, but the Shunemite woman simply replied, "It will be all right."

When we go to our source—the Lord Almighty—every challenge *will be all right*. Elisha raised the Shunemite woman's son from the dead, and God will solve your problems if you go to him.

✗ PRAYER

Dear Lord,

I'm running to you. Give me solutions and fix everything that's broken in my life.

In Jesus' name, amen.

►◄ STRENGTH IN THE WORD

Those who search will surely find me.

PROVERBS 8:17

◄► TODAY I DECLARE

All of God's promises belong to me.

▼ JOURNAL ENTRY

Ask the Lord to resurrect a promise that seems dead.
With faith, go directly to your source.

Journal away!

23. What Did You Say?

WHEN I LISTEN TO CERTAIN NURSERY RHYMES, I wonder, *Who in the world sat on that selection committee?* Case in point: Who came up with "Sticks and stones may break my bones, but words will never hurt me"? Proverbs 18:21 warns, "The tongue can bring death or life; those who love to talk will reap the consequences." Clearly, words *can* hurt!

There is an ancient Jewish legend that tells of a king who gave two jesters a command. In so many words, it goes like this: "Foolish Simon, go and bring me the best thing in the world. And you, Silly John, go and find me the worst thing in the world." Shortly after, each jester returned with a package. Simon said, "Behold, Sire, the *best* thing in the world." He unwrapped his package, and it contained a tongue. Silly John laughed and quickly unwrapped his package. It was also a tongue!

Truly, the tongue is the best thing and worst thing in the world. The story of Zechariah illustrates its power. An angel told Zechariah that his wife, Elizabeth, would have a son—but Zechariah didn't believe the angel. He said, "How can I be sure this will happen? I'm an old man now, and my wife is also well along in years." The angel replied, "Since you didn't believe what I said, you will be silent and unable to speak until the child is born" (Luke 1:5-20).

The angel had to silence Zechariah to keep him from undermining God's plan. Our words have that much power! With a slip of the tongue, we can lose everything. And with the grace of the tongue, we can harvest a life full of blessings.

⏳ PRAYER

Dear Lord,
Forgive me for every
harmful word that
I've spoken.
In Jesus' name, amen.

⌖ STRENGTH
IN THE WORD

The words of the
wise bring healing.

PROVERBS 12:18

⌖ TODAY I DECLARE

I will pause, breathe,
and think before I speak.

Reflect on the circumstances that habitually make you regret the things that you say. How can you avoid these patterns in the future?

Journal away!

* KEEPSAKE
"We can harvest a life full of blessings."

24. Is the Baby Protected?

GOD PLANTS "BABIES" INSIDE EACH OF US in the form of dreams. They begin as embryonic hopes that can grow into full-term realities. But like any developing baby, our dreams must be protected after they're conceived. "Debbie Downer" (your pessimistic friend) probably shouldn't know that you're carrying. "Doubting Thomas" (with little faith) might need to be kept at bay. And "Chatty Cathy" (who tells all your business)—why do you confide in her anyway?

During the early gestation period, dreams easily miscarry due to premature exposure. Think of the dreams you conceived in the past. *Why didn't they see the light of day?* As an entrepreneur, I understand the joy one feels when a new dream is on the horizon. Yet despite your excitement, your "baby" must be protected.

According to Luke 1:5-24, Elizabeth, Zechariah's wife, miraculously conceived their child when she was "very old," and soon after, she "went into seclusion for five months." When I studied this story, two questions came to mind: *Why was seclusion necessary? And why five months?* Clearly, Elizabeth was beyond the normal childbearing age. Few, if any, would have believed that she was carrying a baby—much less a *healthy* one. Imagine the things that people would've said: *"She's delusional." "There's no way it will happen."* (Does any of that sound familiar?) Most fascinating is the significance of five months. Around that point in the gestation period, women typically begin to show. In essence, Elizabeth concealed her pregnancy until her baby was further developed! She didn't give "Debbie Downer," "Doubting Thomas," and "Chatty Cathy" any dangerous opportunities.

So enjoy the excitement as your dream develops, but always remember to protect your "baby."

⚕ PRAYER

Dear Lord,
Send people into my life
who will encourage and
believe in my dreams.
In Jesus' name, amen.

►◄ STRENGTH
IN THE WORD

Pay attention and
learn good judgment.

PROVERBS 4:1

◄► TODAY I DECLARE

I am carrying a beautiful
dream, and it will be born.

Describe the dream that's inside of you.

Journal away!

* KEEPSAKE

"God plants 'babies' inside each of us."

25. What Has Passed Down?

IN 1974, HARRY CHAPIN RELEASED the popular song "Cat's in the Cradle." The song is about a father who spent his son's childhood being too busy for his family. According to the lyrics, the father had "planes to catch and bills to pay," so his son "learned to walk while [he] was away." *Rolling Stone's* readers picked "Cat's in the Cradle" as one of the saddest songs of all time—because the child became a replica of his father. *"He'd grown up just like me,"* the dad grieved. *"My boy was just like me."*

The average family has negative cycles that pass down from generation to generation. One of the most troubling findings is that children of divorcées are more likely to end up divorced themselves. Like cancer and heart disease, a family's dysfunction is often inherited. Therefore, it's our spiritual obligation to tear these cycles down.

Joshua heard God's call to do the same. After leading the Israelites into the Promised Land (Canaan), his first task was to conquer Jericho. The city was surrounded by double walls that were at least thirteen feet tall. The two walls were joined by a smooth, thirty-five-foot plaster slab that sloped upward at thirty-five degrees. It was impenetrable. However, God told Joshua, "I have given you Jericho, its king, and all its strong warriors. . . . The walls of the town will collapse" (Joshua 6:2-5). And they crumbled down.

The same God who tore down the walls of Jericho can dismantle your family's negative cycles. Divorce and substance abuse can be torn down. Lies and lack can be torn down. Whatever it is, God will partner with your faith—and tear it all down.

⚕ PRAYER

Dear Lord,

Carry my family into
the Promised Land, where
dysfunction ceases to
be our destiny.

In Jesus' name, amen.

STRENGTH IN THE WORD

I am about to do
something new. See,
I have already begun!

ISAIAH 43:19

TODAY I DECLARE

No dysfunction will stand.

What negative cycles have you observed in your family?

Journal away!

* KEEPSAKE

"It's our spiritual obligation to tear these cycles down."

26. What Do You Really Want?

HAVE YOU EVER HOPED FOR SOMETHING PRIVATELY, but denied wanting that thing? Like a baby, degree, relationship, or promotion? *"No, I'm happy single,"* some say—but they're secretly longing to be married. *"I couldn't care less if they speak to me,"* another might say—but they really miss their friend.

Research confirms that women are less likely to communicate what they really want. That partly explains why we typically make less in the workplace. According to Linda Babcock, coauthor of *Women Don't Ask,* men are four times more likely to ask for a raise. And when women do ask, they usually request 30 percent less.

The Bible gives every believer—including women—permission to ask for what they desire. In fact, the Parable of the Persistent Widow teaches us to ask—and keep asking—until we receive the things we want.

In the Gospel of Luke, Jesus told his disciples a story about a widow who went to a heartless judge and said, "Give me justice in this dispute with my enemy." For quite some time, the judge simply ignored her. But the widow kept asking. Finally, the judge had endured enough. "He said to himself, 'I don't fear God or care about people, but this woman is driving me crazy. I'm going to see that she gets justice, because she is wearing me out with her constant requests!'" (Luke 18:1-8).

As women, we don't have to suppress or deny our desires. We can be bold and forthcoming. Matthew 7:7 encourages, "Keep on asking, and you will receive what you ask for. Keep on seeking, and you will find. Keep on knocking, and the door will be opened to you."

PRAYER

Dear Lord,

Shape me into a persistent woman. Help me to remain encouraged whenever I'm ignored or told no.

In Jesus' name, amen.

STRENGTH IN THE WORD

You can pray for anything, and if you believe that you've received it, it will be yours.

MARK 11:24

TODAY I DECLARE

I will be honest about what I want.

Describe a time when you were bold and fearless.

Journal away!

* KEEPSAKE
"We can be bold and forthcoming."

ASK FOR WHAT

YOU WANT,

AND BE PREPARED

TO GET IT.

ATTRIBUTED TO MAYA ANGELOU

27. Will You Seek Vengeance?

LIFE IS SOMEWHAT IRONIC. The parent who mistreated you will likely end up needing your care, and the colleague who betrayed you will, perhaps, request a recommendation. Forgiveness is difficult and complicated, but does it require that we turn our cheeks and simply forget?

Without even an apology, forgiveness wipes the slate clean and cancels a debt. It renders mercy when punishment is rightly due. That's what David gave to King Saul. The king was paranoid and jealous, so he tried to kill David: "Saul hunted him day after day, but God didn't let Saul find him." But the king was determined. "Saul chose 3,000 elite troops from all Israel and went to search for David. . . . At the place where the road passes some sheepfolds, Saul went into a cave to relieve himself. But as it happened, David and his men were hiding farther back in that very cave!"

David literally caught Saul with his pants down and could've easily destroyed him. "Now's your opportunity!" his men said. David considered it for a moment, then replied, "The LORD forbid that I should do this to my lord the king." So he restrained his men and didn't attack Saul (1 Samuel 23:14; 24:2-7).

Forgiveness isn't stupidity. It doesn't require that we put ourselves in harm's way. Though David forgave Saul for his treachery, he continued to exercise caution—because he knew what Saul was capable of. Likewise, we shouldn't necessarily forget affronts and wrongdoings, for our memories protect us from future danger. But when we forgive, we no longer calculate (or bring up) what someone has done. We release the offense and leave vengeance to God.

☰ PRAYER

Dear Lord,

Wash away the bitterness and pain that's still in my heart.

In Jesus' name, amen.

►◄ STRENGTH IN THE WORD

Forgive anyone you are holding a grudge against, so that your Father in heaven will forgive your sins, too.

MARK 11:25

◄► TODAY I DECLARE

I'm strong enough to forgive.

▼ JOURNAL ENTRY

Which person do you find most difficult to forgive?
What would you gain if you let the grudge go?

Journal away!

* KEEPSAKE
"Release the offense and
leave vengeance to God."

28. Does It Hurt?

HAVE YOU EVER HAD A TINY PIMPLE? Well, I can tell you from personal experience that they can be dreadful. I mean *absolutely dreadful!* I recently had one that you could barely see. If I wasn't suffering from its torture, I wouldn't have known it was there. How could something so small be so excruciatingly painful? The more I touched it, the more it hurt. The more I thought about it, the more miserable I became. Finally, I just surrendered: The pimple was going to hurt—at least until it dried up.

When someone hurts us, the same principle applies. The more we "touch it" (rehearsing it in our minds and lamenting over it in our hearts), the more painful it becomes. But before positive thinking was a "thing," the Bible taught people to redirect negative thoughts. Philippians 4:8 states, "Fix your thoughts on what is true, and honorable, and right, and pure, and lovely, and admirable. Think about things that are excellent and worthy of praise."

There is also a growing body of research that points to the healing powers of our minds. According to a study conducted at Wake Forest University, positive thinking can be as powerful as a shot of morphine in reducing pain.

By retraining your mind (replacing negativity with positivity), you can soothe what aches. Instead of picking at your "pimple," praise God for everything in your life that *doesn't* hurt. And rather than dwelling on your misery, meditate on the goodness of God: "He will wipe every tear" (Revelation 21:4); "He heals the brokenhearted" (Psalm 147:3); and "[He] will give you back what you lost" (Joel 2:25).

⚊ PRAYER

Dear Lord,

Heal my broken heart
and bandage my wounds.

In Jesus' name, amen.

▸◂ STRENGTH
IN THE WORD

Let the Spirit renew your
thoughts and attitudes.

EPHESIANS 4:23

◂▸ TODAY I DECLARE

I will focus on my
blessings, not my pain.

▼ JOURNAL ENTRY

Describe something that brightens your mood
when you think about it.

Journal away!

* KEEPSAKE
"Meditate on the goodness of God."

29. Too Hard to Love?

BECOMING A CHRISTIAN doesn't make loving people any easier. The same shenanigans that bothered you *before* you were born again may be the same shenanigans that frazzle you *after* you're born again. Some people will always drive you crazy—like folks who use their speaker phones in a public place, and drivers who activate their turn signals . . . *miles* before making an actual turn.

When we accept Jesus Christ through repentance, our minds are made up, but our flesh puts up a fight. You've probably noticed this before: Your mind is determined to "keep the peace" with your relatives, but your flesh rises whenever they push your buttons. In fact, relatives can be the hardest to love. Mother Teresa once stated, "It is not always easy to love those close to us." But in 1 Corinthians 9:27, the apostle Paul admits, "I discipline my body like an athlete, training it to do what it should." Some translations state, "I beat my body" (WEB and NHEB). Even the legendary apostle Paul had to subdue his nature.

Loving people is hard. That's why Jesus named it as the most important commandment after loving God (Mark 12:28-31). A love switch doesn't miraculously turn on because we become born again; we have to manually switch it on. It's a daily, lifelong decision that requires tremendous effort.

Colossians 3:14 encourages, "Above all, clothe yourselves with love." That verse is a soothing reminder that love isn't always organic. It doesn't automatically ooze out of you because you become a Christian. Rather, you must "clothe" yourself in it—put it on, dress in it, and cover your nature.

⌛ PRAYER

Dear Lord,
Give me the strength
to dominate my flesh.
In Jesus' name, amen.

►◄ STRENGTH IN THE WORD

This is my command:
Love each other.

JOHN 15:17

◄► TODAY I DECLARE

I will manually turn
on my love switch.

▼ JOURNAL ENTRY

Write a love declaration that you can recite and "dress yourself in" every morning.

Journal away!

＊ KEEPSAKE

"It's a daily, lifelong decision."

30. Have You Asked?

HAVE YOU HEARD OF A "DECISION SUPPORT SYSTEM"? It's a fancy technological term with a thought-provoking meaning. OxfordDictionaries.com defines it as "a set of related computer programs and the data *required* to assist with analysis and decision-making within an organization."

If we swim through the tech jargon, that definition somewhat describes the Holy Spirit. He is our Chief Advisor, and he gives us the "data" we need to make wise decisions. The Holy Spirit sees what we can't see with our natural eyes. He knows what we don't know with our limited insight. His counsel is also *required*.

When we invite the Holy Spirit into our lives, we no longer carry the burden of figuring out everything on our own. We can ask him for help. In fact, wise people consult the Holy Spirit before making important decisions. What's the point of having an all-knowing, all-seeing, all-powerful Chief Advisor if we don't seek his counsel? *Should you take that job?* Ask the Holy Spirit. *Should you marry that man?* Ask the Holy Spirit. *Should you speak up and say something?* Ask the Holy Spirit. *Should you let go and move on?* Ask the Holy Spirit!

Although he usually doesn't answer with an audible voice (just imagine how terrifying that could be), the Holy Spirit often guides us through Scripture, with a sense of peace, or through a special messenger (such as a friend or pastor). Proverbs 3:5-6 encourages, "Trust in the LORD with all your heart; do not depend on your own understanding. Seek his will in all you do, and he will show you which path to take."

✶ PRAYER

Dear Lord,
Give me the guidance
that I need and show me
which path to take.
In Jesus' name, amen.

►◄ STRENGTH
IN THE WORD

All who are led by the Spirit
of God are children of God.

ROMANS 8:14

◄► TODAY I DECLARE

The Holy Spirit is my Chief
Advisor. I will seek his advice.

▼ JOURNAL ENTRY

Make a list of the decisions that you're currently facing
and ask the Holy Spirit to guide you.

Journal away!

＊ KEEPSAKE

*"The Holy Spirit sees what
we can't see."*

31. Whose Voice Is That?

THERE ARE TWO VOICES THAT COMPETE for our attention: *God's voice and the devil's voice.* Knowing the difference is the most important skill that we can acquire. In Matthew 4, Jesus was led by the Holy Spirit into the wilderness to be tempted by the devil. It was a test for Jesus and a road map for us.

After fasting for forty days and forty nights, Jesus was hungry. Seizing the opportunity, Satan said, "If you are the Son of God, tell these stones to become loaves of bread." In that exchange, the devil tempted Jesus with the "lust of the flesh" (1 John 2:16, NIV). This strategy dangles sin that feeds our physical urges. Sins like gossip, sexual immorality, mean thoughts, and acts of rage. *But God's voice never dangles spiritual poison.*

Satan also took Jesus to the highest point of the Temple and said, "If you are the Son of God, jump off!" The devil tempted Jesus with the "pride of life." He wanted Jesus to believe that—because he was the Son of God—he could force God to protect him. Pride tells us that we're entitled; that we can irreverently make demands. *But God's voice doesn't fatten our egos, nor does it recklessly test God's faithfulness.*

Next, Satan showed Jesus all the kingdoms of the world and said, "I will give it all to you . . . if you will kneel down and worship me." The "lust of the eyes" takes our gaze off God. It entices us to worship things and people. *But God's voice will never ask us to bow down to anything—or anyone—other than him.*

⚡ PRAYER

Dear Lord,
Make your voice
loud and clear.
In Jesus' name, amen.

►◄ STRENGTH
IN THE WORD

Obey his commands, listen
to his voice, and cling to him.

DEUTERONOMY 13:4

◄► TODAY I DECLARE

I will measure every
voice against Scripture.

▼ JOURNAL ENTRY

True or false: I know the sound of God's voice.

Journal away!

* KEEPSAKE

"God's voice never dangles spiritual poison."

32. Did You Hear the Whisper?

HAVE YOU BEEN IN A SITUATION—or met someone—and thought, *I don't know what it is, but something isn't right?* Oftentimes, we quickly dismiss the thought and later find out that our discernment was right.

Contrary to what your inner critic might tell you, discernment isn't *paranoia*; nor is it *judgment*. In the Bible, the concept of discernment is typically translated from two Greek words: *anakrinō* (which means "examine closely") and *diakrinō* (which means "to separate, make a distinction, discriminate"). In essence, when we discern something, we are able to distinguish the good from the bad.

Discernment is the supernatural ability to detect something fishy. It somewhat feels like a gut instinct, but it's actually a subtle message from God that warns us of danger. For example, think of a time when you felt uncomfortable but you weren't sure why. Everything looked good and sounded right, but an internal alarm left you unsettled. That was discernment!

God usually speaks to us through a gentle whisper. If you're waiting for a cacophonous alarm to go off, you'll be disappointed. In 1 Kings 19, when the prophet Elijah was in trouble, God didn't speak to him in the windstorm, earthquake, or fire that appeared (verses 11-13). Instead, the Lord spoke to the prophet through a whisper—and God speaks to us through the gentle whisper of the Holy Spirit. So the next time you sense that something isn't right, don't ignore it. Use your gift of discernment to distinguish the good from the bad. Listen to God's whisper.

PRAYER

Dear Lord,

Sharpen my spiritual discernment. Develop my ability to detect and perceive.

In Jesus' name, amen.

STRENGTH IN THE WORD

I believe in your commands; now teach me good judgment and knowledge.

PSALM 119:66

TODAY I DECLARE

I won't judge or condemn, but I will listen and discern.

Create a list of options (like parks, beaches, or nooks) where you can go to hear from God. Each location can be a designated "discerning space."

Journal away!

* KEEPSAKE
"Discernment isn't paranoia; nor is it judgment."

33. How Do You Talk to Yourself?

TALKING TO YOURSELF CAN SEEM A BIT NUTTY, but research confirms that it's good for your soul. Self-talk—the conversations that we have *with* ourselves *about* ourselves—calms anxiety and makes things more clear. Plus, it's biblical!

The sons of Korah frequently encouraged themselves as if they were encouraging someone else. Psalms 42:5, 11 and 43:5 repeat these uplifting words: "Why, my soul, are you downcast? Why so disturbed within me? Put your hope in God, for I will yet praise him, my Savior and my God" (NIV).

A study conducted by psychologists Ethan Kross and Jason Moser revealed that during self-talk, people who refer to themselves in the third person rather than the first person have an easier time dealing with stressful situations. For example, instead of Sandra's saying, "*God will supply my needs,*" it would be better for her to say, "*Sandra, God will supply your needs.*" Also, treating ourselves as if we're other people changes the dialogue from being self-critical to self-encouraging. This is vital—because we're typically less compassionate with ourselves. Job cried out, "Even if I were innocent, my mouth would condemn me; if I were blameless, it would pronounce me guilty" (Job 9:20, NIV).

Therefore, minister to yourself as if you're uplifting someone else. Speak gentle words of advice and encouragement: "*Sandra, you're strong enough to overcome this difficult season.*" "*You're brave enough to face your fears.*" Motivational speaker and fellow believer Zig Ziglar once said, "The most influential person who will talk to you all day is you, so you should be very careful about what you say to you."

⏳ PRAYER

Dear Lord,

Teach me how to uplift myself.

In Jesus' name, amen.

►◄ STRENGTH IN THE WORD

Let everything you say be good and helpful, so that your words will be an encouragement to those who hear them.

EPHESIANS 4:29

◄► TODAY I DECLARE

I will be my greatest cheerleader.

▼ JOURNAL ENTRY

If you could go back in time and talk to your younger self,
what would you say?

Journal away!

＊ KEEPSAKE
"Minister to yourself."

34. Are You Martha?

MARTHA OF BETHANY OFTEN GETS A BAD SHAKE. Mary, her sister, sat at Jesus' feet and soaked up his teaching while Martha frenzied over making her big dinner. But why was Mary's choice the "better" choice (Luke 10:42, NIV)? Didn't Jesus appreciate good old-fashioned hospitality?

The Gospel of Luke recounts, "As Jesus and the disciples continued on their way to Jerusalem, they came to a certain village where a woman named Martha welcomed him into her home. Her sister, Mary, sat at the Lord's feet, listening to what he taught. But Martha was distracted by the big dinner she was preparing. She came to Jesus and said, 'Lord, doesn't it seem unfair to you that my sister just sits here while I do all the work? Tell her to come and help me.'

"But the Lord said to her, 'My dear Martha, you are worried and upset over all these details! There is only one thing worth being concerned about. Mary has discovered it, and it will not be taken away from her'" (Luke 10:38-42).

As a busy bee myself, I feel Martha's pain. Why couldn't Jesus give her an "atta-girl" for her efforts? Wasn't it *Martha* who welcomed him into her home and fed his swarm of disciples? *But herein lies the problem:* Martha's desire to serve was stronger than her desire to be in the presence of the Lord. Although her intentions were probably good, Martha's busyness became her god!

Some of us fall into the "Martha trap"—doing a million commendable things, but failing to spend enough time with the Lord. But be careful when it comes to the busyness of life. *Working* for Christ is different from *knowing* Christ.

⌛ PRAYER

Dear Lord,
Give me a heart that finds
genuine joy by simply
sitting in your presence.
In Jesus' name, amen.

►◄ STRENGTH
IN THE WORD

Seek the Kingdom
of God above all else.

MATTHEW 6:33

◄► TODAY I DECLARE

Knowing God is
my priority.

If you had a face-to-face moment with God,
what do you think he'd say to you?

Journal away!

✳ KEEPSAKE
*"Working for Christ is different
from knowing Christ."*

35. Do You Give Honor?

THERE'S A STORY IN THE BIBLE that has always befuddled me. From guilt-ridden laughter to serious concern, my reactions have run the gamut. But after years of making light of the story, the seriousness has struck me.

The prophet Elisha was walking along a road, and a group of boys started to tease him. "Go away, baldy!" they chanted. It wasn't a nice thing to say, but no biggie, right? They were kids just playing games. *Well, here's what happened next:* "Elisha turned around and looked at them, and he cursed them in the name of the LORD. Then two bears came out of the woods and mauled forty-two of them." Yes, you read that correctly! Elisha caused the death of forty-two kids! But the craziest part might be the next sentence: "From there Elisha went to Mount Carmel and finally returned to Samaria" (2 Kings 2:23-25). The passage continues as if nothing happened!

For years, I've been amused by this story (pardon my dark humor), and I've wondered why the account was even included in the Bible. Was it intended to reveal Elisha's temper, or was it included to merely illuminate the craziness of the times? *Possibly neither.* The account of the boys might simply drive home the importance of honoring spiritual authority. No one gets a pass—not even children.

God didn't reprimand Elisha for his actions, because God sanctioned them. He was a man of God who deserved honor. In today's world, few think twice before showing disrespect. However, the story of Elisha and the boys is a warning: We must give honor to those in spiritual authority—and we better teach our kids to do the same.

☥ PRAYER

Dear Lord,

Forgive me for any dishonor
I have thought or shown.

In Jesus' name, amen.

►◄ STRENGTH
IN THE WORD

Honor those who are your
leaders in the Lord's work. . . .
Show them great respect.

1 THESSALONIANS 5:12-13

◄► TODAY I DECLARE

I will give honor
wherever honor is due.

▼ JOURNAL ENTRY

Be intentional about honor. Which leaders in your
life deserve more honor from you?

Journal away!

* KEEPSAKE

"No one gets a pass."

36. Where Is the Compassion?

IN HIS BOOK *THE NAME OF GOD IS MERCY,* Pope Francis shares a story about an Argentinian mother. After being abandoned by her husband, the woman prostituted herself to feed her children. One day, she asked to speak with Father Jorge Bergoglio, which is Pope Francis's birth name. He assumed that she wanted to thank him for a shipment of goods that were sent.

"Did you receive it?" Father Bergoglio asked.

"Yes, thank you for that, too," the woman replied. "But I came here today to thank you because you never stopped calling me Señora."

Compassion is the extension of love, no matter what someone has done. It's the act of rendering mercy when it's in your power to withhold it. Joseph of Nazareth is a wonderful example.

Mary and Joseph were engaged to be married, "but before the marriage took place, while [Mary] was still a virgin, she became pregnant through the power of the Holy Spirit" (Matthew 1:18). At this point in the story, Joseph wasn't aware of the immaculate conception that occurred. He understandably concluded that Mary was (to put it lightly) "fast and loose." Even in that frame of mind, Joseph showed her compassion. Verse 19 states, "Joseph, to whom she was engaged, was a righteous man and did not want to disgrace her publicly, so he decided to break the engagement quietly."

The waitress (who deserves to be fired) is likely going through a rough season. The person who cut you off—then gave you a birdie—may be on the brink of a breakdown. And that "unbearable" colleague is probably *unbearably* unhappy. We can all do the world a favor by taking a long, compassionate, deep breath.

꩜ PRAYER

Dear Lord,
You turn the hearts of
kings, so turn mine
toward compassion.
In Jesus' name, amen.

►◄ STRENGTH IN THE WORD

Be compassionate, just as
your Father is compassionate.

LUKE 6:36

◄► TODAY I DECLARE

Compassion is the heartbeat
of my everyday ministry.

▼ JOURNAL ENTRY

Think of an interaction that didn't go well. If you had a do-over, how would you show more compassion?

Journal away!

✳ KEEPSAKE

"Take a long, compassionate, deep breath."

37. Are You Sincere?

THE PHRASE *I'M SORRY* is used for a variety of reasons. It can mean "I'm sorry ... (I got caught)," "I'm sorry ... (only to shut you up)," or "I'm sorry ... (so you can't say I'm not sorry)." Disingenuous apologies sometimes work with people, but they never work with God.

Repentance is the act of genuine contrition (regret for doing wrong). The biblical Greek word translated as "repentance" is *metanoia*. It means to have a "change of heart" or "change of mind"—to move forward in a different direction.

Josiah became king of Judah when he was eight years old. Though he was totally committed to God, he didn't know about the Book of the Law, which the high priest discovered in the Temple during the eighteenth year of Josiah's reign. Upon learning what was written, Josiah tore his clothes in despair. He then ordered his officials, "Speak to the LORD for me and for the people and for all Judah.... We have not been doing everything it says." So they consulted with the prophetess Huldah, and she sent this message to Josiah on behalf of God: "You were sorry and humbled yourself.... You tore your clothing in despair and wept before me in repentance. And I have indeed heard you, says the LORD" (2 Kings 22:1-19).

God accepted Josiah's repentance because it was sincere. When the king learned of his wrongdoing, he immediately sought to correct his behavior—and we must do the same. We can't intentionally sin and halfheartedly repent. God sees into our hearts. Therefore, *genuinely* seek the Lord and move forward in the right direction. "I'm sorry" doesn't work when we deliberately make the same mistakes.

PRAYER

Dear Lord,

Forgive me for my lack of sincerity. Help me change my heart and mind.

In Jesus' name, amen.

STRENGTH IN THE WORD

Repent of your sins and turn to God.

ACTS 3:19

TODAY I DECLARE

Now that I know better, I will do better.

▼ JOURNAL ENTRY

Have you ever thought or said, *"Lord, forgive me for what I'm about to do"*?

Journal away!

＊ KEEPSAKE

"God sees into our hearts."

38. Is Forgiveness Too Free?

OUR CULTURE TEACHES US to undervalue things that are easily acquired. If we're handed something that's free, we generally question it. *Is it damaged? Is it tainted? Is it low-grade?* We're conditioned to reject any possibility of getting something valuable for nothing. Maybe that's why people struggle with accepting God's forgiveness. It's simply too free.

In the Bible, Naaman had a similar issue. He was a warrior who suffered from leprosy. It must have been unsightly, because his wife's maidservant recommended that he go to the prophet Elisha to be healed. *What happened next might surprise you.*

When Naaman arrived at Elisha's door, the prophet sent a messenger with these instructions: "Go and wash yourself seven times in the Jordan River. Then your skin will be restored, and you will be healed of your leprosy." Oddly, Naaman became angry! It all seemed too simplistic.

"I thought [Elisha] would certainly come out to meet me!" Naaman said. "I expected him to wave his hand over the leprosy and call on the name of the LORD his God and heal me!" But when Naaman did as Elisha had told him, "his skin became as healthy as the skin of a young child." Adding to Naaman's bewilderment, Elisha refused to accept a gift in return (2 Kings 5:1-19).

To Naaman, the healing process was too simple and too free. But God healed him anyway. Naaman's reaction might seem ridiculous, yet we sometimes respond the same way. Instead of accepting God's free and simple forgiveness, we hold on to our guilt and shame. However, Jesus already paid the price for our sins. There's no lingering debt. "It is finished!" Jesus said (John 19:30).

☒ PRAYER

Dear Lord,

Forgive my sins and wash me clean. I accept your free grace.

In Jesus' name, amen.

►◄ STRENGTH IN THE WORD

When he was hung on the cross, he took upon himself the curse for our wrongdoing.

GALATIANS 3:13

◄► TODAY I DECLARE

I am forgiven.
Jesus paid the price.

▼ JOURNAL ENTRY

Jot down two Scriptures that you can recite when guilt and shame reappear. Then journal about what makes them powerful.

Journal away!

_____

_____

_____

_____

_____

_____

_____

_____

_____

_____

_____

_____

_____

_____

_____

_____

_____

_____

_____

_____

* KEEPSAKE
"There's no lingering debt."

39. Are Strings Attached?

CHURCH FOLKS ARE GENERALLY FAMILIAR with at least some variation of Luke 6:38: "Give, and you will receive. Your gift will return to you in full—pressed down, shaken together to make room for more, running over, and poured into your lap." This Scripture is often quoted to entice people to give, and it generally works during offerings. But the Lord opened my eyes during one of my not-so-perfect moments.

I was upset because I thought I had gone "above and beyond" for an ungrateful friend. (*Has that happened to you?*) When the person didn't thank me, my love turned into resentment. At first I was in denial. *Maybe he's just busy. He'll get around to it.* Then my denial turned into self-pity, and my pity party progressed into bitterness. *After all that I did, how could he not thank me?* I even blamed God: *Lord, how could you allow this person to treat me like this?* These feelings went on for months.

One day while sitting in my car, the truth hit me like a freight train: I was giving with strings attached. When I gave love, I expected love in return. When I gave respect, I required respect in return. When I gave friendship, I looked for friendship in return. In my heart, there were conditions.

Although Luke 6:38 promises that God will reward us, a reward should never be the reason why we give. It should merely be the perk! We ought to love because God first loved us, and we must give because God first gave to us.

⚡ PRAYER

Dear Lord,

Purify my heart, so I can give without conditions.

In Jesus' name, amen.

▶◀ STRENGTH IN THE WORD

Humanly speaking, it is impossible. But with God everything is possible.

MATTHEW 19:26

◀▶ TODAY I DECLARE

I will continue to give, even if the favor isn't returned.

▼ JOURNAL ENTRY

Are you harboring resentment toward an ungrateful friend or relative? Search your heart and release the conditions.

Journal away!

---

* KEEPSAKE

"We must give because God first gave to us."

IT'S NOT HOW MUCH WE GIVE,

BUT HOW MUCH LOVE

WE PUT INTO GIVING.

ATTRIBUTED TO MOTHER TERESA

40. Is It Your Business?

THERE'S A BUSYBODY IN ALMOST EVERY CHURCH and family. They meddle in other people's affairs and poke around in places where they don't belong. Busybodies are called a lot of names, like "nosy parker," "snoop," and "rubbernecker," but my favorite might be "scandalmonger."

Busybodies love a good scandal. The juicier the better: *"Did you hear about Sally's divorce? Girl, all that glitters isn't gold! Two affairs, a baby on the side, and her husband's marrying the new mistress! Sweet Jesus! I'll be praying for them. I already told Anisa, Tracy, Wilma, and Becky we all need to pray."*

Busybodies can't see themselves. They're blinded to the venom that they spew. They're convinced that they're "helping," but the Bible classifies them with criminals. Consider 1 Peter 4:15-16, which warns, "If you suffer . . . it must not be for murder, stealing, making trouble, or prying into other people's affairs." Murderers are grouped with busybodies, and the comparison makes sense. Busybodies slaughter reputations, slay relationships, and kill self-esteems.

The next time you feel inclined to "help," ask yourself these three questions:

1. *Is this any of my business?*
2. *Has God given me this assignment?*
3. *Have those involved asked for my help?*

The wrong answers are obvious. As believers, we must evict the busybodies that live within us, and (with love) we must confront the busybodies who live among us. "Urge them in the name of the Lord Jesus Christ to settle down. . . . Don't think of them as enemies, but warn them as you would a brother or sister" (2 Thessalonians 3:12-15).

☼ PRAYER

Dear Lord,
Help me take a long,
courageous look in the
mirror. Show me myself.
In Jesus' name, amen.

►◄ STRENGTH
IN THE WORD

Interfering in someone else's
argument is as foolish as
yanking a dog's ears.

PROVERBS 26:17

◄► TODAY I DECLARE

I will mind my business and
keep gossip from my lips.

▼ JOURNAL ENTRY

The next time someone approaches you with a juicy piece
of gossip, what will you say?

Journal away!

✳ KEEPSAKE

"Busybodies can't see themselves."

41. Why Compare?

FROM VERY EARLY IN LIFE, we're taught to compare ourselves to other people. If we're not careful, our entire lives can bounce from one comparison to another: *Who ranks the highest in school? Who has the happiest marriage? Who is the most successful?* Even as little girls we recited, *"Mirror, mirror, on the wall, who's the fairest of them all?"* However, it's important to recognize that sizing yourself up to others will only lead to a negative outcome. You will either think more highly of yourself than you ought (Romans 12:3) or be riddled with insecurities because you think that you don't measure up.

If you wrestle with comparisons, you're in respectable company. The apostle Peter had a similar challenge. When Jesus revealed that Peter would die a martyr, Peter wasn't satisfied with merely knowing his destiny; he also wanted to know John's. The Bible recounts, "Peter turned around and saw behind them the disciple Jesus loved [John]. . . . Peter asked Jesus, 'What about him, Lord?' Jesus replied, 'If I want him to remain alive until I return, what is that to you? As for you, follow me'" (John 21:15-22).

God has declared a unique calling over your life, and it requires that you follow *him*—rather than your comparisons. You might think that "Susan" has the perfect life, but it wouldn't be perfect *for you.* When God crafted your purpose, he did it with your gifts and character in mind. *So, why compare?* Galatians 6:4 teaches, "Pay careful attention to your own work, for then you will get the satisfaction of a job well done, and you won't need to compare yourself to anyone else."

⚊ PRAYER

Dear Lord,

Keep my eyes on you. Remove pride and envy from my heart.

In Jesus' name, amen.

►◄ STRENGTH IN THE WORD

In his grace, God has given us different gifts for doing certain things well.

ROMANS 12:6

◄► TODAY I DECLARE

God has a unique and beautiful plan for my life.

▼ JOURNAL ENTRY

What do you admire most about yourself? Don't be bashful.

Journal away!

_____

_____

_____

_____

_____

_____

_____

_____

_____

_____

_____

_____

_____

_____

_____

_____

_____

_____

_____

_____

_____

_____

_____

_____

_____

_____

_____

✻ KEEPSAKE

"God has declared a unique calling over your life."

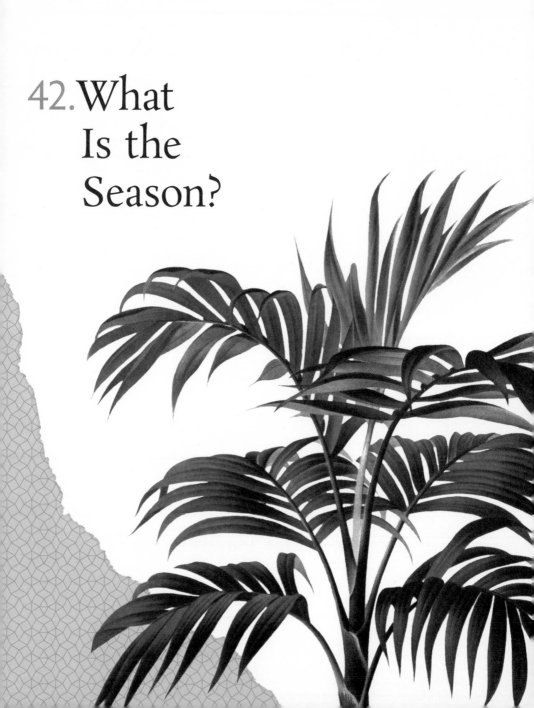

42. What Is the Season?

OUR LIVES ENCOMPASS MANY DIFFERENT SEASONS. Like kiwis in the winter and apricots in the spring, God empowers us to bear seasonal fruit. That might explain the struggle to meet "Mr. Right" during a "career-building season," and why it's tough to launch a dream during a "season of rest." Ecclesiastes 3:1 teaches, "For everything there is a season, a time for every activity under heaven."

Seasons provide the ideal conditions for bearing certain types of fruit. But if you're focused on a season other than the one that you're in, you'll miss the harvest that's right in front of you.

When David was in the "season of shepherding," he gave it everything that he had. His commitment yielded invaluable skills—which God later used to slay Goliath. Furthermore, when David was in the "season of serving," he didn't pine over becoming king. Instead, he served Saul with all his heart—and thereby cultivated the fruit of loyalty among the Israelites: "Whatever Saul asked David to do, David did it successfully. So Saul made him a commander . . . an appointment that was welcomed by the people" (1 Samuel 18:5).

It might feel like you're unable to produce in your current season, but you can! If you're in the "season of motherhood," bask in the time that you have with your children. You're sowing seeds that will bloom throughout their lives. And if you're in the "season of singlehood," savor the opportunity to invest in yourself. A woman who isn't married "can be devoted to the Lord" (1 Corinthians 7:34). So whatever season you're in, enjoy the fruit that it yields—because seasons don't last forever.

⚮ PRAYER

Dear Lord,

Open my eyes to the beauty of this season. Water my seeds and let them bear fruit.

In Jesus' name, amen.

►◄ STRENGTH IN THE WORD

I am planting seeds of peace and prosperity among you.

ZECHARIAH 8:12

◄► TODAY I DECLARE

I will maximize and find joy in my current season.

▼ JOURNAL ENTRY

Name your current season and itemize the types
of fruit that it can yield.

Journal away!

* KEEPSAKE

*"God empowers us to bear
seasonal fruit."*

43. Will You Take This Blessing?

READING THE SONG OF SOLOMON can make good Christian girls blush. Even the slightly naughty ones, like me, turn a bit red. The verses can get really steamy. A good chunk of them make you look around—just to check if someone is peeking over your shoulder. *Have you read these?* "Your breasts are like two fawns, twin fawns of a gazelle grazing among the lilies. . . . You are altogether beautiful, my darling, beautiful in every way" (4:5-7). Those verses are hot and romantic!

The Word of God illuminates the power of marital sex. Its sensual virtues *gratify* (Proverbs 5:19), *bond* (Genesis 2:24), *comfort* (2 Samuel 12:24), and *reproduce* (Genesis 4:1). But like all types of power, sex is often misused.

Some women—*even Christian women*—use sex as a weapon. If their husbands don't do what they prefer, they render punishment by withholding "the goods."

In the Bible, the matter was so grave that the apostle Paul addressed it with the Corinthians: "Do not deprive each other of sexual relations, unless you both agree to refrain from sexual intimacy for a limited time so you can give yourselves more completely to prayer. Afterward, you should come together again" (1 Corinthians 7:5). In the midst of preaching on "weightier" issues, the apostle Paul addressed sex. It was that important of an issue.

Through the power of sex, marriage can satisfy a myriad of needs. So, don't use sex as a weapon. *Indulge* in the steamy blessings it was created for.

⚱ PRAYER

Dear Lord,

Let me experience
every blessing—
spiritual and sensual.

In Jesus' name, amen.

►◄ STRENGTH IN THE WORD

The husband should fulfill
his wife's sexual needs, and
the wife should fulfill her
husband's needs.

1 CORINTHIANS 7:3

◄► TODAY I DECLARE

My power will be a
blessing, not a weapon.

▼ JOURNAL ENTRY

Who's your favorite Bible couple? Jacob and Rachel?
Hannah and Elkanah? Esther and King Xerxes?

Journal away!

* KEEPSAKE
"*The Word of God illuminates the power of sex.*"

44. Are You Intentionally Intimate?

WHEN PEOPLE THINK OF INTIMACY, they often think of sex. But people can have sex without being intimate—and people can be intimate without having sex. *Intimacy* involves emotional closeness, privacy, and trust; however, *love* is defined as "patient and kind" (1 Corinthians 13:4). It is unselfish. Intimacy is much different from love. Love should be freely given, but intimacy should be earned.

Women tend to be relational beings. At times, we share way too much about our feelings, dramas, and traumas—with anyone we befriend and anyone who will listen. However, Proverbs 4:23 cautions, "Guard your heart above all else, for it determines the course of your life." This Scripture is primarily about guarding our hearts from *sin*, not from *people*. But the central message emphasizes that our hearts should be protected. We ought to be intentional about *what* we share and *how much* we share.

Jesus was cautious when it came to intimacy. He appointed twelve apostles, but only Peter, James, and John witnessed his Transfiguration (Jesus' most transparent state; Luke 9:28-36). And only Peter, James, and John saw Jesus agonizing in the garden of Gethsemane (Jesus' most vulnerable state; Matthew 26:36-46). Our Savior didn't share everything with everyone. He was intentional.

As you continue to build relationships, routinely ask yourself, *Am I being intentional about what I share?* Your BFF doesn't need to know everything about your hubby or beau—nor does your mother or hairstylist! And that awesome idea you have? Everyone won't understand it, so everyone shouldn't know the details about it. Therefore, love freely—love generously—but, like Jesus, be intimate wisely.

PRAYER

Dear Lord,

Show me which people
to confide in and trust.

In Jesus' name, amen.

STRENGTH
IN THE WORD

If you need wisdom, ask our
generous God, and he will
give it to you.

JAMES 1:5

TODAY I DECLARE

I will be intentional
about what I share.

▼ JOURNAL ENTRY

Has the Holy Spirit warned you about a certain friend, colleague, or relative? Explore how you can love that person generously, while avoiding intimacy.

Journal away!

* KEEPSAKE
"Intimacy should be earned."

45. Have You Embraced the Process?

URING ONE OF *CALLED* MAGAZINE'S photo shoots in Philadelphia, a publicist once said to me, "This is impressive!" I must have been exhausted because I overlooked the compliment and gave her a way-too-transparent reply: *"Anything that I now do right, it's because I once did it wrong."* I suppose "Thank you" would have sufficed. But on that day, I didn't sugarcoat the truth. The fact was, the Lord had taken me through an arduous training process. Even though he always carried the bulk of the weight, there were days—possibly months—maybe years—when I was barely holding on. I learned by stumbling and fumbling along the way. I guess that's why it's called "growing pains."

History teaches that success is sweet, but it doesn't *just happen*. It requires that we continuously grow. In the Bible, Joseph was seventeen years old when God gave him a dream—but that dream wasn't fulfilled until twenty-three years later. Joseph had to go through the process of preparation. He acquired wisdom through the *process* of being sold into slavery by his brothers; he grew in faith through the *process* of being falsely accused by Potiphar's wife; he refined his character through the *process* of being thrown into prison; and he developed patience through the *process* of being forgotten by the chief cup-bearer. These experiences prepared Joseph for the call on his life.

For Joseph, it took twenty-three years for his dream to be realized. For you, it might take five years, fifteen years, or even more. However long it takes, God is with you—every step of the way—training and molding you through his process.

PRAYER

Dear Lord,

Shape me according to your perfect will, and give me the strength to endure the process.

In Jesus' name, amen.

STRENGTH IN THE WORD

The LORD was with Joseph, so he succeeded in everything he did.

GENESIS 39:2

TODAY I DECLARE

I will yield to the Lord's training process.

▼ JOURNAL ENTRY

How is God preparing you? Write down the trials that are making you stronger and wiser.

Journal away!

* KEEPSAKE

*"God is with you—
every step of the way."*

46. Is He Absent?

I N THE BIBLE, God is never mentioned by name in the book of Esther. Terms like *Yahweh*, *Elohim*, and *Adonai* aren't anywhere. This interesting fact has led some scholars to question whether the book of Esther belongs in the canon of Scripture. According to Karen Jobes, an esteemed Bible scholar, not one commentary was written on Esther during the first seven centuries of the Christian church. It was believed that the absence of God's name meant the absence of his presence. Oddly, when you read the story of Esther, a Jewish orphan who became Queen of Persia, it's hard to imagine that God isn't mentioned. His voice is almost deafening in its silence—particularly in the protection of Mordecai, Esther's cousin.

When Haman, the most powerful official in King Xerxes's empire, "saw that Mordecai would not bow down or show him respect, he was filled with rage. . . . So he decided it was not enough to lay hands on Mordecai alone. Instead, he looked for a way to destroy all the Jews throughout the entire empire." But one night, the king had trouble sleeping. And he ordered that the court records be read to him. In those records, the king discovered that Mordecai had once saved his life by exposing a brewing assassination attempt. Subsequently, the king honored Mordecai and intercepted Haman's villainous plan (Esther 3:5–7:10).

From chapter to chapter, the hand of the Lord is working behind the scenes in the book of Esther. The same is true in our lives. God may be silent, but his presence is real. The Lord's invisible hand is fighting your battles, ordering your steps, and keeping a King awake on your behalf.

⚱ PRAYER

Dear Lord,

Let me feel your presence and sense your invisible hand.

In Jesus' name, amen.

►◄ STRENGTH IN THE WORD

[The LORD] will neither fail you nor abandon you.

DEUTERONOMY 31:6

◄► TODAY I DECLARE

God is with me. He's working things out on my behalf.

▼ JOURNAL ENTRY

What special song helps you feel God's presence?
Write down the lyrics.

Journal away!

※ KEEPSAKE

"God may be silent, but his presence is real."

47. Will You Pick Yourself Up?

EVERYONE GOES THROUGH THE BLUES at one point or another. There's no escaping them. In a strange way, the blues serve as excellent mentors. They teach you how to be resilient when life knocks you down.

Many men and women of the Bible suffered from the blues when things got tough. Though their faith was strong, they were human—just like us. In 1 Samuel 1, Hannah grieved her inability to conceive a child. Her sorrow ran so deep that she wouldn't eat. "Why are you crying, Hannah?" her husband, Elkanah, would ask. "Why aren't you eating? Why be downhearted just because you have no children? You have me—isn't that better than having ten sons?" (Now that's a loving man!)

The prophet Elijah also sang his set of the blues, because crazy Jezebel was determined to kill him. "'I have had enough, LORD,'" he said. 'Take my life, for I am no better than my ancestors who have already died.' Then he lay down and slept under the broom tree. But as he was sleeping, an angel touched him and told him, 'Get up and eat!' . . . So he ate and drank" (1 Kings 19:4-6).

Depression is a serious condition that requires professional help; however, the blues are normal human emotions that we can climb above. They're triggered by real-life challenges, and they fade when those challenges are overcome.

If you are feeling the blues, you can choose to pick yourself up. When David was greatly distressed, he encouraged himself in the Lord (1 Samuel 30:6). David reminded himself of God's goodness, faithfulness, and provision. You can do the same. And while you're at it, "get up and eat" like Elijah.

PRAYER

Dear Lord,

Turn my mourning into dancing and my troubles into joy.

In Jesus' name, amen.

STRENGTH IN THE WORD

Here on earth you will have many trials and sorrows. But take heart, because I have overcome the world.

JOHN 16:33

TODAY I DECLARE

Sadness will not consume me. I'll pick myself up and choose joy.

▼ JOURNAL ENTRY

List the things that bring you real joy. Whenever you're feeling the blues, indulge in those joyful pleasures.

Journal away!

* KEEPSAKE

"Be resilient when life knocks you down."

48. Should You Try Another Way?

ONE NIGHT WHILE PREPARING FOR BED, I was putting rollers in my hair *(the soft ones that actually allow you to sleep)*. But for some reason, I got stuck in one spot. I kept trying to roll a particular corner, but it wouldn't work. Either the hair would slip out, the roller wouldn't close, or I would roll the hair in the wrong direction. The frustrating episode went on for about fifteen minutes. Just when I was about to give up, a thought occurred to me: *Reposition your arms.* So I lifted my arms above my head. And *voilà!* It worked.

There will be moments when we think that something can't work—because it hasn't *yet* worked. We will tell ourselves that "it's not meant to be" or "it's not possible." But God doesn't want us to quit that easily. Consider the biblical story of the paralyzed man. Jesus was teaching, and people showed up from every village in Galilee and Judea, and from Jerusalem as well. "And the Lord's healing power was strongly with Jesus."

Seeing an opportunity, the friends of a paralyzed man "tried to take him inside to Jesus, but they couldn't reach him because of the crowd. So they went up to the roof and took off some tiles. Then they lowered the sick man on his mat down into the crowd, right in front of Jesus." *(Wouldn't it be wonderful if we all had friends like that?)* Jesus healed the man, and "everyone was gripped with great wonder" (Luke 5:17-26).

The friends of the paralyzed man refused to give up. When one approach didn't work, they adjusted their strategy. Therefore, don't quit so easily when things seem impossible. Reposition yourself and try another way.

⚓ PRAYER

Dear Lord,

Increase my capacity to be a creative problem-solver. Help me try new and better ways.

In Jesus' name, amen.

►◄ STRENGTH IN THE WORD

I can do everything through Christ, who gives me strength.

PHILIPPIANS 4:13

◄► TODAY I DECLARE

When things seem impossible, I won't give up so easily.

▼ JOURNAL ENTRY

What difficult situation or seemingly impossible dream are you
ready to give up on? Do you feel led to try a different approach?
Explore what you can do differently.

Journal away!

* KEEPSAKE
*"Reposition yourself and
try another way."*

49. What Is Joy?

RICHARD WURMBRAND, a Romanian pastor, was imprisoned for fourteen years because he wouldn't stop preaching the gospel. In his bestseller, *Tortured for Christ*, Wurmbrand describes how he was beaten, burned, locked in an icebox, and kept in solitary confinement for three years.

"It was strictly forbidden to preach to other prisoners, as it is in captive nations today," he wrote. "It was understood that whoever was caught doing this received a severe beating. A number of us decided to pay the price for the *privilege* of preaching, so we accepted their terms. It was a deal: we preached and they beat us. We were happy preaching; they were happy beating us—so everyone was happy."

Joy isn't what we think it is. It's not the jolly, carefree, "everything is great" feeling that we're sold in commercials. Joy is the unwavering happiness that we experience when we're partnered with God's plan. Some of us will struggle financially and give sacrificially, but we'll feel joy because we're changing lives. And many moms will be professionally sidelined and emotionally overwhelmed, but they'll find joy in raising their children.

As believers, we can choose joy despite our difficulties. The apostle Paul wrote, "Our hearts ache, but we always have joy. We are poor, but we give spiritual riches to others. We own nothing, and yet we have everything" (2 Corinthians 6:10). Joy—unexplainable delight—persists when we're living with purpose in the trenches with God. There's endless joy when we remember why we live—and embrace the *privilege* of serving the God we live for.

PRAYER

Dear Lord,
Let your unwavering,
unexplainable joy
consume my life.
In Jesus' name, amen.

STRENGTH IN THE WORD

When troubles of any kind
come your way, consider it an
opportunity for great joy.

JAMES 1:2

TODAY I DECLARE

Nothing can steal my joy.

▼ JOURNAL ENTRY

Name something in your life that was worth the struggle.
What joy did the challenge bring?

Journal away!

* KEEPSAKE

*"We can choose joy despite
our difficulties."*

50. Have You Given Thanks?

LOVE COFFEE LIKE MICE LOVE CHEESE. It's a serious love affair. One morning, I made the perfect batch. It was heaven in a cup. Sipping with my eyes closed, I was in my "happy place." *Then it suddenly happened:* The cup tipped, and my happy liquid started to spill. Jolted, I quickly grabbed the cup and whispered, *"Thank you, Lord. All isn't lost."*

As long as we still have life, we can give thanks because our cup isn't empty. God always makes something beautiful out of whatever we have left. In 1 Thessalonians 5:18, the apostle Paul encourages, "Be thankful in all circumstances, for this is God's will for you who belong to Christ Jesus." This means we should embrace gratitude through whatever we face.

The legend of chef George Crum teaches that we should be thankful when we face difficulties. In his upscale kitchen at Moon's Lake House, Crum prided himself on the ability to "'take anything edible and transform it into a dish fit for a king.'" But on a frustrating day in 1853, an uppity diner disagreed. Crum's potatoes were too thick, too soggy, and too bland, the patron stated. So Crum indignantly made a new batch that was paper thin, fried to the crunch, and heavily salted. Thus, the potato chip was born! Crum's frustration birthed a brilliant recipe.

God causes *all things* to work together for our good (Romans 8:28), including our spills, difficulties, and frustrations. That's why we ought to give thanks! Spilled coffee is a reminder that all isn't lost; a troubled marriage reveals God's healing power; a difficult season draws us closer to the Lord; and a frustrating situation can birth new levels of creativity.

⏳ PRAYER

Dear Lord,

Thank you for every
experience in my life.
In Jesus' name, amen.

►◄ STRENGTH IN THE WORD

We give thanks to you,
Lord God, the Almighty.

REVELATION 11:17

◄► TODAY I DECLARE

Everything is working
toward my ultimate good.

▼ JOURNAL ENTRY

Count your blessings! Create a gratitude list, and don't
forget the challenges that made you better.

Journal away!

---

* KEEPSAKE

*"We can give thanks because
our cup isn't empty."*

51. Will You Win or Lose?

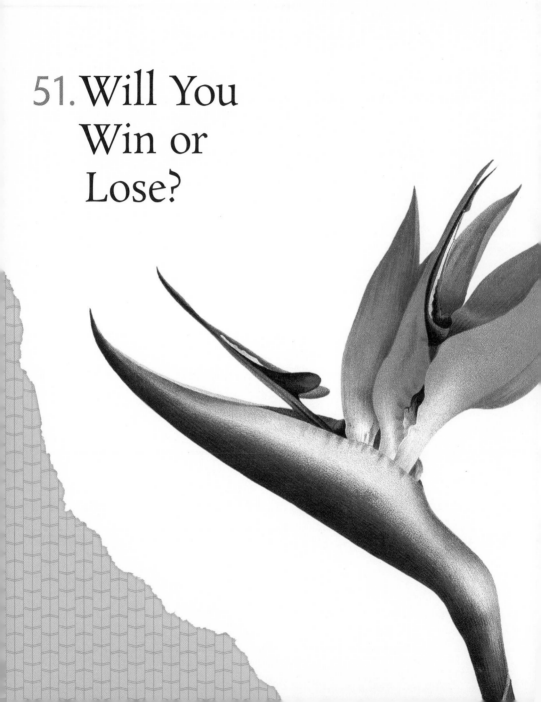

W HEN PEOPLE ARE UNITED, very little can stop them. That's why Satan works hard to "kill and destroy" relationships. That's his purpose (John 10:10).

In Matthew 18:19, Jesus promised, "If two of you agree here on earth concerning anything you ask, my Father in heaven will do it for you." Concerning *anything*? Have you ever wondered why Jesus made such a bold, blanket statement? Maybe because people seldom agree— on *anything*! They can be in the same marriage, same church, and same partnership—yet be divided against each other.

In the Kingdom of God, we are one body made up of many unique parts. "The eye can never say to the hand, 'I don't need you.' The head can't say to the feet, 'I don't need you'" (1 Corinthians 12:21). In fact, unity is so powerful that God gave us different languages to temper it. Genesis 11:1 states, "At one time all the people of the world spoke the same language and used the same words." They were of one mind. Subsequently, they put their skills together and decided to build a great city, along with a tower that reached heaven. But the Lord noticed and said, "Look! . . . The people are united, and they all speak the same language. After this, nothing they set out to do will be impossible for them!" (verse 6).

Every day, we're in a spiritual battle to remain united; however, God's soldiers are often unaware of the fight. We surrender to broken relationships without considering the greater mission at stake. Our true enemy is the devil, not each other. He's battling behind the scenes to keep us divided—because united we win, but divided we lose.

ꙮ PRAYER

Dear Lord,

Give me a spirit that binds
people together. Transform
me into an agent of peace.
In Jesus' name, amen.

►◄ STRENGTH
IN THE WORD

A town or family splintered
by feuding will fall apart.

MATTHEW 12:25

◄► TODAY I DECLARE

Peace and harmony will reign
in my family and friendships.

▼ JOURNAL ENTRY

List five ways you can strengthen one of your relationships.

Journal away!

✳ KEEPSAKE

"United we win, but divided we lose."

52. What Are You Waiting For?

WHENEVER I HAVE A PROJECT THAT I'D RATHER NOT DO, I feel motivated to do all sorts of *other* things. Suddenly, the kitchen pantry needs to be organized, and every toilet needs to be scrubbed. Then I notice the mountain of e-mails in my in-box and the laundry that's calling my name. That's the beauty of procrastination: Everything—except the important thing—gets done.

James Albery, an English playwright, wrote an epitaph that highlights the dangers of dillydallying:

> He slept beneath the moon,
> He basked beneath the sun;
> He lived a life of going to do
> And died with nothing done.

Graveyards are full of callings that people never got around to answering—procrastination is that cunning of a thief. It steals time. It tells us that we can put things off. But the "perfect" moment may never come: Motivation might always be low; money might always be tight; and life might always be busy. However, Ecclesiastes 11:4 warns, "Farmers who wait for perfect weather never plant. If they watch every cloud, they never harvest."

Have you ever wondered why women have babies, considering the pain of labor? It can be an unpleasant experience, but mothers keep the end result in mind. Completing your life's mission "will be like a woman suffering the pains of labor. When her child is born, her anguish gives way to joy because she has brought a new baby into the world" (John 16:21). So "push" through the cunning schemes of procrastination and keep the end result in mind. There's something beautiful waiting to be born.

PRAYER

Dear Lord,

Bless me with the will to get things done, with or without motivation.

In Jesus' name, amen.

STRENGTH IN THE WORD

Don't put it off; do it now!

PROVERBS 6:4

TODAY I DECLARE

If it should be done now, it will be done now.

▼ JOURNAL ENTRY

What important project are you putting off?
List the benefits of getting it done.

Journal away!

* KEEPSAKE
*"There's something beautiful
waiting to be born."*

NOTES

1: **WHAT DOES IT MEAN?**
"Abolitionist William Lloyd Garrison called Harriet the 'Moses' of her people." "Harriet Tubman, the Moses of Her People," Harriet Tubman Historical Society, accessed February 21, 2019, http://www.harriet-tubman.org/moses-underground-railroad/.

2: **DO YOU ACCEPT THE DEFINITION?**
"'He will cause pain.'" Alfred Jones, *Jones' Dictionary of Old Testament Proper Names* (Grand Rapids, MI: Kregel, 1997), s.v. "Jabez."

3: **ARE YOU BOUND?**
"But that's what Aron Ralston did…" See J. Michael Kennedy, "CMU Grad Describes Cutting Off His Arm to Save His Life," *Pittsburgh Post-Gazette*, May 9, 2003, http://old.post-gazette.com/nation/20030509climbernat2.asp.

6: **IS LAZARUS DEAD?**
"began her painting career in her mid-seventies"; "painted thousands of creations—including 25 after the age of 100"; "various reproductions have been placed on…fabrics, tiles, and greeting cards." See "On This Day: Grandma Moses Is Dead at 101; Primitive Artist 'Just Wore Out,'" *New York Times* on the Web Learning Network, December 14, 1961, https://archive.nytimes.com/www.nytimes.com/learning/general/onthisday/bday/0907.html.
"various reproductions have been placed on china"; "In 1946, 16 million of her Christmas cards were sold." See "'Curious' Art of Grandma Moses," *Washington Times*, March 19, 2001, https://www.washingtontimes.com/news/2001/mar/19/20010319-021647-8319r/.
"one of her paintings was purchased for $1.2 million in 2006." See "Grandma Moses," artnet, accessed November 15, 2018, http://www.artnet.com/artists/grandma-moses/biography.

7: **WHAT DOES GOD THINK OF WOMEN?**
"Blessed art Thou…" Maimonides, "The Mishneh Torah, Chapter 7," trans. Moses Hyamson, Sefaria, accessed December 10, 2018, https://www.sefaria.org/Mishneh_Torah%2C_Prayer_and_the_Priestly_Blessing.7.6?ven=The_Mishneh_Torah_by_Maimonides._trans._by_Moses_Hyamson,_1937-1949&lang=bi, emphasis added.

9: **HAVE YOU MADE REST A PRIORITY?**
"A 2016 report indicated that since 2010, Chick-fil-A had led the fast-food industry in average sales per restaurant." Michael Furick, "Transferring Competitive Advantage into International Markets: Chick-fil-A Case Study," *Journal of Business and Economics* 7, no. 5 (May 2016): 829, doi: 10.15341/jbe(2155-7950)/05.07.2016/010, http://www.academicstar.us/UploadFile/Picture/2016-10/2016101154434330.pdf.

10: **CAN GOD INVEST IN YOU?**
"At the age of nineteen months, Helen Keller…" *Encyclopaedia Britannica*, s.v. "Helen Keller," last modified October 5, 2018, https://www.britannica.com/biography/Helen-Keller.

13: **HOW HEAVY IS THE LOAD?**
"They simply got too heavy, according to a New Zealand study." See Charles Q. Choi, "Why Ostriches Can't Fly," LiveScience, January 28, 2010, https://www.livescience.com/8055-ostriches-fly.html.

16: **IS THE GATE GUARDED?**
"Gatekeepers played an important role…" See "What Was the Significance of Gatekeepers in the Bible?" Got Questions, accessed November 15, 2018, https://www.gotquestions.org/gatekeepers-in-the-Bible.html.
"After God's people returned from exile in Babylon…" See 1 Chronicles 9:1-2, 22, 28-29.

17: **IS IT A BOWL OF STEW?**
"Warren Buffett once gave up billions…" Matthew Frankel, "Warren Buffett's Worst Investment of All Time Will Shock You," The Motley Fool, October 5, 2016, https://www.fool.com/investing/2016/10/05/warren-buffetts-worst-investment-of-all-time-will.aspx.

19: **IS IT A DISTRACTION?**
"It takes approximately twenty-five minutes to return to a task after being interrupted, says Gloria Mark, a researcher at the University of California, Irvine." See Bob Sullivan and Hugh Thompson, "Brain, Interrupted," *New York Times*, May 3, 2013, https://www.nytimes.com/2013/05/05/opinion/sunday/a-focus-on-distraction.html.

25: **WHAT HAS PASSED DOWN?**
"Cat's in the Cradle" lyrics. "Harry Chapin—Cat's in the Cradle Lyrics," METROLYRICS, accessed November 15, 2018, http://www.metrolyrics.com/cats-in-the-cradle-lyrics-harry-chapin.html.
"Rolling Stone's readers picked 'Cat's in the Cradle' as one of the saddest songs of all time." See "Readers' Poll: The 10 Saddest Songs of All Time," October 2, 2013, *Rolling Stone*, https://www.rollingstone.com/music/music-lists/readers-poll-the-10-saddest-songs-of-all-time-10875/1-eric-clapton-tears-in-heaven-208829/.

"children of divorcées are more likely to end up divorced themselves." See Renée Peltz Dennison, PhD, "Are Children of Divorce Doomed to Fail?" *Psychology Today*, August 2, 2014, https://www.psychologytoday.com/us/blog/heart-the-matter/201408/are-children-divorce-doomed-fail.

"The city was surrounded by double walls that were at least thirteen feet tall." John F. Guilmartin, *Encyclopaedia Brittanica*, s.v. "Military technology," accessed January 23, 2019, https://www.britannica.com/technology/military-technology.

"The two walls were joined by a smooth, thirty-five-foot plaster slab that sloped upward at thirty-five degrees." Danielle Park, "Wall of Jericho," Civil Engineer/Online Historical Database of Civil Infrastructure, accessed February 1, 2019, https://www.thecivilengineer.org/online-historical-database-of-civil-infrastructure/item/393-wall-of-jericho.

26: WHAT DO YOU REALLY WANT?
"According to Linda Babcock, coauthor of Women Don't Ask ..." Joanne Lipman, *That's What She Said: What Men Need to Know (and Women Need to Tell Them) about Working Together* (New York: William Morrow, 2018), 120.

28: DOES IT HURT?
"According to a study conducted at Wake Forest University ..." "Positive Thinking a Pain Reliever," BBC News, September 5, 2005, http://news.bbc.co.uk/2/hi/health/4215078.stm.

29: TOO HARD TO LOVE?
"It is not always easy to love those close to us." Caitlin O'Connell, "12 Powerful Mother Teresa Quotes That Will Stay with You," *Reader's Digest*, accessed November 19, 2018, https://www.rd.com/true-stories/inspiring/mother-teresa-quotes/.

30: HAVE YOU ASKED?
"a set of related computer programs ..." *OxfordDictionaries.com*, s.v. "decision support system," accessed December 5, 2018, https://en.oxforddictionaries.com/definition/decision_support_system, emphasis added.

31: WHOSE VOICE IS THAT?
"lust of the flesh"; "pride of life"; "lust of the eyes." See 1 John 2:16, NIV.

32: DID YOU HEAR THE WHISPER?
"anakrinō (which means 'examine closely')." *StudyLight.org*, s.v. "ἀνακρίνω," Liddell-Scott-Jones Definitions, no. 1, accessed November 26, 2018, https://www.studylight.org/lexicons/greek/350.html.

"diakrinō (which means 'to separate, make a distinction, discriminate')." *BibleHub*, s.v. "1252. diakrinó," Thayer's Greek Lexicon, no. 1, accessed November 26, 2018, https://biblehub.com/greek/1252.htm.

33: HOW DO YOU TALK TO YOURSELF?
"A study conducted by psychologists Ethan Kross and Jason Moser ..." See "The Weird Way of Talking That Can Help with Stress," Yahoo! LIFESTYLE, July 27, 2017, https://www.yahoo.com/lifestyle/weird-way-talking-can-help-stress-182000604.html.

"The most influential person who will talk to you all day is you, so you should be very careful about what you say to you." Zig Ziglar, *Over the Top* (Nashville: Thomas Nelson, 1997), 68.

36: WHERE IS THE COMPASSION?
"In his book The Name of God Is Mercy, Pope Francis shares a story ..." Pope Francis, *The Name of God Is Mercy: A Conversation with Andrea Tornielli*, trans. Oonagh Stransky (New York: Random House, 2016), 60–61. See also Maral Shafafy and Ande Wanderer, "Pope Francis: Argentina's Homegrown Holy Leader," wander-argentina, accessed November 26, 2018, https://wander-argentina.com/pope-francis-argentinas-pope/.

37: ARE YOU SINCERE?
"The biblical Greek word that's translated as 'repentance' is metanoia." *BibleHub*, s.v. "3341. metanoia," accessed November 27, 2018, https://biblehub.com/greek/3341.htm; *Merriam-Webster.com*, s.v. "metanoia," https://www.merriam-webster.com/dictionary/metanoia.

46: IS HE ABSENT?
"According to Karen Jobes, an esteemed Bible scholar, not one commentary was written on Esther during the first seven centuries of the Christian church." Karen H. Jobes, *The NIV Application Commentary: Esther* (Grand Rapids, MI: Zondervan, 1999), 21.

49: WHAT IS JOY?
"It was strictly forbidden ..." Richard Wurmbrand, *Tortured for Christ: 50th Anniversary Edition* (Colorado Springs: David C Cook, 2017), 58, emphasis added.

50: HAVE YOU GIVEN THANKS?
"The legend of chef George Crum ..." Pamela Cyran and Chris Gaylord, "The 20 Most Fascinating Accidental Inventions," *Christian Science Monitor*, October 5, 2012, https://www.csmonitor.com/Technology/2012/1005/The-20-most-fascinating-accidental-inventions/Potato-chips.

52: WHAT ARE YOU WAITING FOR?
"James Albery, an English playwright ..." *Osmania Veterinarian, Vol. 2* (Hyderabad, India: Osmania University, 1954), 52.

ABOUT THE AUTHOR

M ARSHA DuCILLE is the founder and editorial director of *CALLED* magazine, the largest North American–based publication for Christian women. Her "hobby turned global venture" reaches women worldwide through a variety of multimedia platforms. She is also the creative director of CALLED Design, a print and digital solutions enterprise; the creative principal of CALLED Boutique, a merchandising brand; and the chairman of The CALLED Project, a philanthropic arm that supports outreach efforts around the world. Marsha earned a master's degree in social work from Boston University and a master's degree in educational foundations, research, and policy from the University of Michigan.